THE GHOST HUNTER'S HANDBOOK

The Ghost Hunter's Handbook

Cornwall

ANNIE HENSHAW

Sphinx House

CONTENTS

Also by Annie Henshaw:
Narrowboating for Novices

Heritage Railways & Tramways of the British Isles

Sphinx House
Norfolk, PE30 3QB

INTRODUCTION

All the locations listed in these pages are accessible to the public. One or two buildings have been included which are not open to the public but whose haunted areas (eg a court-yard or a window) are visible from public land.

Where the story behind the ghost of a particular location is known, this is given in full. However, in some cases little has been reported other than that the place is haunted. If you learn something new about a haunted location please let us know and we'll endeavour to include it in the next edition of the book.

In order to help you to plan your trip, brief information about the facilities provided by listed inns and hotels is included.

This is the first volume in a series of Ghost Hunter's Handbooks. If you would like to be informed when other volumes are published – and to learn of any special offers – please contact us at info@sphinxhouse.com with the word 'Ghost' in the subject line.

MAP SHOWING APPROXIMATE POSITIONS OF HAUNTED LOCATIONS OPEN TO THE PUBLIC IN CORNWALL

(numbers correspond to those in the listing of locations)

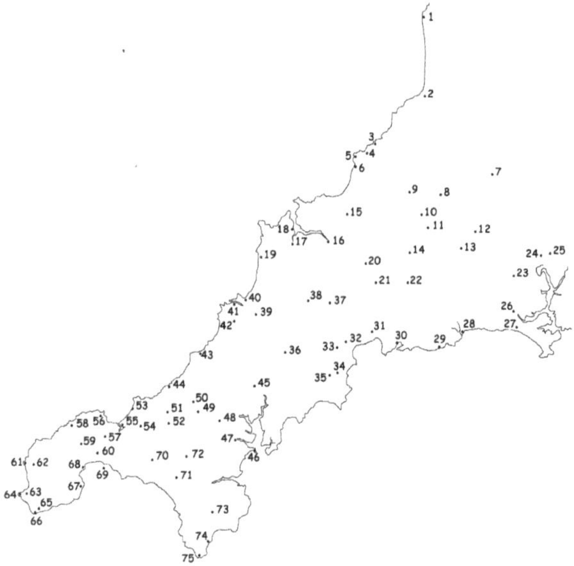

1. MORWENSTOW

1a. The Church of St Morwenna and St John the Baptist

Morwenstow is the most northerly village in Cornwall and its ghost stories mainly revolve around one man – the Reverend Robert Stephen Hawker – who, from 1834 to 1875, was the vicar of the parish church of St Morwenna and St John the Baptist.

The church, which is now a Grade I listed building, has Norman origins. Parts were added on in the 13th, 15th and 16th centuries. Restoration was undertaken in the 1850s by the Reverend Hawker. The most recent restorations took place in the early 20th century.

Often referred to as Parson Hawker, the vicar was an eccentric man who preferred colourful clothes to the traditional black clerical garb, kept nine cats and a pet pig, and built for himself a little shack on the cliffs where he would sit for hours writing hymns and poetry. This shack now has the distinction of being the smallest property owned by the National Trust. Hawker is also remembered as the creator of the modern form of the Anglican harvest festival service.

The vicarage that Hawker took over when he arrived in Morwenstow was fairly dilapidated so he decided to replace it with a new one - with a skyline as eccentric as himself. One of the chimneys is in the form of his mother's tomb, and the rest are modelled on the towers of churches where he had previously worked.

One thing to which Parson Hawker was committed was giving a Christian burial to sailors who drowned as a result of shipwrecks in the area. The graveyard of the parish church has over 50 such burials. A figurehead retrieved from the sailing ship Caledonia which ran aground in 1842 marks the burial place of the crew who died.

Even on his deathbed, Parson Hawker displayed some eccentricity by converting to Roman Catholicism after a lifetime of serving the Anglican church. This had rather sad consequences as it meant that he could not be laid to rest next to his late wife in St Morwenna's churchyard but instead had to be buried in Ford Park Cemetery in Plymouth.

THE GHOSTS OF ST MORWENNA'S CHURCH AND CHURCHYARD

In the churchyard, many people have reported seeing the ghosts of sailors – no doubt, those who are buried there.

The colourful figure of Parson Hawker has been seen standing in the churchyard, near his wife's grave, and footsteps (presumed to be his) have been heard in the church. He has also been encountered walking along the nearby country lanes towards the church.

Interestingly, considering the amount of time that he spent there, Parson Hawker has not been seen in his shack. However, pipe smoke and a sweet smell (possibly that of the opium which he smoked in later life to try to counteract depression) have both been smelled there. Many people are aware of an 'atmosphere' in the shack – although some feel euphoric while others feel depressed, possibly reflecting his different moods at different times.

The Church of St Morwenna and St John the Baptist
Morwenstow EX23 9SR

1b. The Bush Inn

As with many coastal inns in Cornwall, the ghosts at the Bush Inn seem to be mostly those of sailors who died when their ships were wrecked nearby. One of these sailors has been seen standing at the foot of the staircase and his footsteps are often heard around the inn. Another sailor – an older man – likes to materialise in one of the bedrooms and sit on the bed. A group of people has been observed from time to time on the stairs – but if anyone speaks to them, they vanish.

Whether it was these ghosts playing games or whether another entity was responsible is unclear but one landlord had a problem with a particular door, which was always left closed overnight and was constantly found open in the morning – even after being wired shut.

The Bush Inn
Crosstown
Morwenstow EX23 9SR

'*phone:* 01288 331242

website: www.thebushinnmorwenstow.com/

email: thebushmorwenstow@outlook.com

The inn serves food and has four bed and breakfast rooms and a self catering apartment in a converted pottery. Free WiFi is available.

2. THE CHURCH OF ST WINWALOE, POUNDSTOCK

In the mid 14th century this church was the site of a murder. The victim, William Penfound, was the curate (or, in other versions of the story, the parish clerk), and he was killed in the chancel by a group of armed men. But no one knows for sure exactly why he was killed – or even when the murder took place. Some stories say that it happened after mass, when the congregation had left and William was alone in the church. Others say that he was killed during mass, in front of the whole congregation. Some sources say it happened in 1356, others say it was a couple of days after Christmas in 1357.

There seem to be four theories as to why William was butchered in this way. The first suggests that the murderers belonged to the Lollard movement – people who saw the clergy as exclusive, corrupt and greedy, and who advocated having the Bible printed in English so that lay people could have a greater opportunity of understanding and taking part in their own religion.

The second theory blames a feud between two local families and says that William was murdered because he had connections to the Lords of Penfound Manor.

The third puts some of the blame on William himself, saying that he was a member of a gang of local pirates (pirates being common in the area) but that he fell out with the others in the gang.

The fourth theory is the direct opposite of the third and says that William was killed because, being a law-abiding man, he had spoken out against local pirates or smugglers.

Records show that two men, John Bevill and Simon de St Gennys, were arrested for the murder on the orders of Edward the Black Prince, and were imprisoned in Launceston Castle. However, their family connections meant that they were only convicted of outlawry, for which they were fined. No one was ever convicted of the murder.

THE GHOST OF THE CHURCH OF ST WINWALOE

William has been seen in the churchyard and by the altar, standing or kneeling in front of it, close to the spot on which he was murdered.

The Church of St Winwaloe
Poundstock EX23 0AX

3. BOSCASTLE

Boscastle is a very pretty village built around a natural harbour with cliffs on either side. It made headline news in August 2004 when the entire village was affected by a severe flash flood and it is famous for its unique and fascinating Museum of Witchcraft and Magic which houses the world's largest collection of occult artefacts. Perhaps it was the popularity of the museum that decided locals to start running a 'Dark Gathering' which has been held annually on Hallowe'en since 2014. The event consists of processions, storytelling, music, and performances by 'dark' morris dancers and 'obby osses'.

Occult symbols are not confined to the village itself. Two miles away, labyrinth-like stone carvings have been found in Rocky Valley. It has been suggested that these were used by local witches to induce altered states of consciousness.

3a. The Old Mill

Dating from the mid 19th century when it ground the corn for the Bos Castle Estate, the mill still retains one of its original water wheels. The story goes that a miller who worked here hid something valuable somewhere in the building and was later murdered, although whether this was as a result of his hiding whatever it was is not clear.

THE GHOST OF THE OLD MILL

The miller's ghost has been seen frequently, especially in the basement where he disappears into a wall. He is instantly recognisable because he has (as in life) only one eye. His disembodied footsteps are also heard around the mill.

Boscastle Old Mill
The Harbour
Boscastle PL35 0AQ
'phone: 01840 250230

The mill now contains a variety of shops.

3b. The Harbour

There are two huge breakwaters in Boscastle harbour and they can be difficult for boats to navigate.

Two ghosts – a man and a middle aged woman – have been seen here, either of whom will be there one minute and gone the next. Who they are no one knows but it is possible that they are the ghosts of people who drowned in the harbour.

3c. The Church of St Symphorian

The church of St Symphorian lies about half a mile south of Boscastle. The legend associated with it tells of the rivalry between St Symphorian's and the church of St Materiana in Tintagel, about five miles to the north. The story became well known thanks to Morwenstow's Reverend Robert Stephen Hawker (see section 1a above) who wrote a poem about it.

The rivalry was all about church bells. Boscastle has the only natural harbour in the 40 mile stretch of coast between Hartland in the north and Padstow in the south. But its church had no bells, so sailors approaching the harbour would listen for the sound of St Materiana's bells to guide them in. These bells were said to have special powers – the people of Tintagel even claimed that they could keep the plague at bay. So, eventually, the citizens of Boscastle decided that they, too, needed church bells. A petition was sent to the church council who, in turn, petitioned the local landowner, Sir William Botreaux. Sir William agreed to commission three bells from John Wickham, a bell maker living in London. (Hawker's account differs at this point, saying that the bells were to come from Spain.)

A ceremony was planned in which St Materiana's bells would ring out as soon as the ship carrying Boscastle's new bells was sighted. In due course, the ship appeared and the bells began to ring. But without warning the sky clouded over and a sudden storm drove the ship onto the cliffs. And, as the ship was wrecked, onlookers heard the new bells ringing out.

Reverend Hawker embellishes the story somewhat. According to him, the only survivor of the wreck was a Cornish fisherman who had been acting as the ship's pilot. He told people that, on hearing the bells of Tintagel, he got down on his knees and thanked God for a safe passage. However, the ship's captain told him that the thanks were due to him, his ship and the calm seas, not to a non-existent deity – at which point the storm began.

The bells were never recovered from the wreck and no further attempt was made to commission bells for the church. The tower of St Symphorian's is still known as 'the silent tower of Botreaux'. As for Sir William Botreaux, it is said that, with no bells to protect him, he died later from the plague. This, however, is probably poetic licence, since the last outbreak of plague in Cornwall was in the mid 17th century whereas the tower of St Symphorian's church, where the bells were to have been housed, was not built until a hundred years later.

THE GHOSTLY BELLS OF FORRABURY CHURCH

Some local people say that you can hear the bells at night, when the sea is very calm. But Hawker, in his poem, says that you can hear them when the sea is stormy. Perhaps the thing to do is just to stand on the clifftop and listen.

The Church of St Symphorian
Forrabury PL35 0DJ

3d. The Napoleon Inn

This 16th century inn is said to have been a recruiting office for the French during the Napoleonic wars. The large number of smugglers in the area made it inevitable, perhaps, that they would want to fight for the country that supplied them with brandy and other highly saleable goods, rather than for the country that was trying to stop them from plying their very profitable trade. Indeed, Adam Smith in his book *The Wealth of Nations* (first published in 1776) described a smuggler as someone who "would have been, in every respect, an excellent citizen, had not the laws of his country made that a crime which nature never meant to be so".

THE GHOST OF THE NAPOLEON INN

Referred to by the locals as 'Plucker', the resident ghost has been known to move things around and to make pictures fall off the walls. He has been seen standing near the fireplace in the bar and some people have felt him pulling at their arms or their clothes. Plucker seems to dislike change and, on one occasion after some redecoration had taken place, he expressed his disapproval by removing a pile of coins from the safe and stacking them on the bar counter. He has also been known to shut the proprietor into a utility room – and turn the key on her.

The Napoleon Inn
High Street, Boscastle PL35 0BD

'phone: 01840 250204

website: www.napoleoninn.co.uk/

The inn serves food. Free WiFi is available.

3e. The Wellington Hotel

It is appropriate, perhaps, that an English village with an inn named after Napoleon should also have a hotel named after Napoleon's great adversary, the Duke of Wellington, although the Wellington Hotel only received this name after the Duke's death in 1852, having previously been called the Bos Castle Hotel. Dating back to the 16th century, it is one of the oldest coaching inns in Cornwall and is said to be one of the most haunted places in Britain. It is now a Grade II list building and in the past its guests have included Guy Gibson (leader of the Dambusters raid), the novelist Thomas Hardy and members of the Royal family.

THE GHOSTS OF THE WELLINGTON HOTEL

If you stay at the Wellington Hotel in the hope of seeing ghosts, ask to be booked into room nine. This is said to be the most haunted part of the hotel and guests have reported shadowy figures, cold blasts of air and an elderly woman standing by the bed late at night. One person even said that the elderly woman pinned her to the bed for about half a minute.

If room nine isn't available, you might want to ask for room 15, 16 or 17, in each of which a semi-transparent little girl has been seen. She has also been seen skipping down the corridor near these rooms. She's a friendly child and has been known to smile at guests before disappearing through a wall.

But it's not just these rooms that are haunted. Ghosts have been seen in many parts of the building. An elderly lady (possibly the same one who visits room nine) has been reported to walk through walls and closed doors. A man who has been seen in the reception area wearing a frilly shirt and black frock coat, with his hair tied back, is thought to have been a coachman who lost control of his horses and plunged into the harbour, where he drowned. However, although he likes to watch people from the shadows, if he is noticed he will walk away and may disappear through a wall.

The ghost of a young woman, who is said to have committed suicide by jumping off the hotel tower after she had been crossed in love, has also been seen drifting around. She tends to materialise on the landing near the top of the tower and may appear either as a misty shape or as completely solid.

A man who is believed either to have been murdered or to have committed suicide has been seen around the hotel, as has a dark shape that floats down the stairs and into the cellar late at night. And it seems that one of the ghosts is a dog lover! One dog, staying in the hotel, wagged his tail in excitement while his owner was aware of an indistinct shape moving across the room. And another dog was reported to have been taken out of the room by a ghostly figure.

The novelist Thomas Hardy and his wife stayed at the

hotel frequently and their ghosts have been seen walking arm in arm around the hotel and in the grounds.

The Wellington Hotel
Old Road
Boscastle PL35 0AQ
'phone: 01840 250202
website: www.wellingtonhotelboscastle.com/
email: info@wellingtonhotelboscastle.com

The hotel has 14 bedrooms, 3 suites, a bar and a restaurant.

4. ST NECTAN'S GLEN

Said to be one of the most spiritual sites in the UK, St Nectan's Glen is a one mile stretch of woodland on the banks of the Trevillet River. At the top of the glen is St Nectan's Kieve (kieve means 'basin' in the Cornish language). This sixty foot waterfall is thought to be the only one of its kind, where the water falls through a hole in the stone into the basin below. The water is said to have healing properties. Also in St Nectan's Glen is a pair of labyrinths carved into the rock. Only just over an inch wide, these are thought to be some 4000 years old.

St Nectan, after whom the glen is named, was said to have been born around the middle of the 5th century, the oldest son of Brychan, king of the Welsh. As a young man he sailed to north Devon where he built a church and hermitage before moving on to Cornwall. He is believed to have built a second hermitage just above the waterfall in what was to become St Nectan's Glen. Legend says that he possessed a silver bell which he would ring during stormy weather when ships were in danger of being wrecked on the coast. But a short time before his death he threw the bell into the kieve, saying that he would never again ring it for unbelievers.

There are several legends as to how he died. The

commonest says that he was beheaded by robbers who were stealing a cow given to him by a local farmer. Undaunted, he picked up his head and walked back to the hermitage! Another legend says that, after his death, two women (possibly his sisters) buried his body beneath the waterfall. The two women continued to live at the hermitage until they, in turn, died and were buried nearby by the villagers.

In his book *An Illustrated Itinerary of the County of Cornwall* (published in 1842), Cyrus Redding tells the story of two other ladies who appeared suddenly in the glen (which he calls "St Nighton's Keive") and moved into the hermitage. From their accents, it was clear that they weren't Cornish, and from the way they dressed they were obviously ladies of quality, but nothing more was known about them. Redding wrote that they lived in the glen for many years, taking "nothing but food from those who inhabited the neighbourhood" . Eventually one died and the other pined away. It is said that they were buried in the glen by the villagers, still as mysterious as they were when they first arrived.

THE GHOSTS OF ST NECTAN'S GLEN

Hooded monks are frequently seen along the glen but other spectral apparitions may be seen or heard, including a man and two women (thought to be St Nectan and his sisters).

Some people have seen an elderly man with a stoop standing by the water. Others have seen a little fire appearing and then vanishing near the second bridge, while one person heard whispering voices and then saw a burning human skull in a tree.

On stormy nights you may hear St Nectan's bell – the one he dropped into the kieve. At other times you may be aware of sobbing or laughter or monastic chanting – or even organ music – as you approach the kieve.

Two 'grey ladies' are thought to be the ghosts of the two elderly ladies whose story Cyrus Redding tells in his book. They have been encountered by a number of people along the path leading to the kieve.

There are also reports of dogs and cats reacting to something that remains invisible to the people around. So if you take your dog with you, don't be surprised if he begins to bark at something or unexpectedly starts to wag his tail!

St Nectan's Glen
Trethevy
Tintagel PL34 0BG

The glen is popular with visitors and, while there is no charge for the woodland walk, you have to pay to see the kieve and hermitage. Sensible shoes are essential because the path is rocky and, even in summer, the ground can be slippery. There is a large parking area on the main Tintagel to Boscastle road (B3263).

5. TINTAGEL

There have been people living in Tintagel since late Roman times and, between the 5th and 7th centuries, it is thought to have been an important trading post. In the 12th century (before the present castle was built) Geoffrey of Monmouth declared in his *History of the Kings of Britain* that King Arthur was conceived here – and the connection with Arthur has remained firmly established since then.

The present castle (now in ruins) dates from around 1230 and was built by Richard, Earl of Cornwall, the second son of King John. The bridge connecting the castle to Tintagel Head was opened in 2019. On Tintagel Island there are the remains of a Celtic monastery. A tunnel running under Tintagel Island is known as Merlin's Cave and legend says that Merlin's voice can sometimes be heard in there.

Legend also says that Condolden Barrow which overlooks Tintagel Island contains the grave of Queen Isolde (of Tristan and Isolde fame) but it is more likely that the person buried there is Cador who was King of Cornwall in the 6th century. Cador has a place in Arthurian legend, having been described by Geoffrey of Monmouth as the sword bearer at Arthur's coronation and as Guinevere's guardian. A 12th century poem describes him as being one of Arthur's knights.

5a. Tintagel Castle

According to Geoffrey of Monmouth, towards the end of the Roman period the British throne was claimed by Uther Pendragon whose father, Constantine, had been king before him. Uther was enamoured of Ygerna, the wife of Gorlais who owned Tintagel Castle. Merlin cast a spell on Uther, changing him to look like Gorlais so that he could make love to Ygerna. And as a result, Arthur was conceived. Some Arthurian scholars believe that Tintagel and Camelot were one and the same.

THE GHOSTS OF TINTAGEL

It is said that in Merlin's Cave you may catch a glimpse Merlin himself and may hear him speaking in a foreign language, as yet unidentified.

Tintagel Castle
PL34 0HE

To visit the castle, you will need to park in Tintagel village and then walk half a mile to Tintagel Head and across the bridge. The pathway tends to be uneven, so sensible shoes are a good idea.

5b. The Old Post Office

This 14th century farmhouse, with its cottage garden and wavy slate roof, was only a post office (or 'letter receiving station') for a brief period during the 19th century. However, the name has stuck.

It was acquired by the National Trust in 1903 – one of its earliest acquisitions.

THE GHOST OF THE OLD POST OFFICE

Some years ago, the National Trust Custodian of the Old Post Office found that, when she turned on the lights each morning, they would flicker, stopping just before she opened the building to the public. Perhaps it was the presence in the Post Office of a machine once used to send telegrams in a form of morse code (known as a Spagnoletti undulator) that led her to wonder whether a message was being transmitted. She tried using the machine to 'interpret' the flickers and found that what was being spelled out was a name – either Nora or Noah. Some further research revealed that a Mrs Noah once lived in the building.

Visitors have reported being aware of Mrs Noah's presence and some have seen her – one visitor was quite taken aback to see a ghostly old lady lying in a bed in the upstairs room.

The Old Post Office

Fore Street , Tintagel PL34 0DB

'phone: 01840770024
website: www.nationaltrust.org.uk/tintagel-old-post-office
email: tintageloldpo@nationaltrust.org.uk

5c. The Camelot Castle Hotel

The hotel itself has three ghosts and there is another nearby, connected to a cottage that was once owned by an engineer who worked at the hotel.

Reviews on TripAdvisor comment on the number of paintings around the hotel. These are obviously irresistable for one of the ghosts who seems to delight in knocking them off the walls. Another of the ghosts is thought, by her behaviour, to have been a nurse since she wakes people up in the night and seems to want to give them a bed bath! The third phantom is usually encountered around the back of the hotel, by the rubbish bins, where people have reported seeing rubbish being thrown out of the bins by unseen hands.

The phantom engineer has often been seen walking along the path from his cottage on his way to work at the hotel. The owner of the hotel has described him as "friendly and harmless". The cottage was bought in 2001 by actress Kate Winslet but she never lived there and eventually she sold it again. Then, in 2012, the cottage burned down and it was suggested locally that it was the ghost, unhappy about all these changes, who had caused the fire. The cottage is now uninhabited but people who have walked past it on dark nights, or when the moon is just rising, have reported seeing ghostly lights shining through its windows.

The Camelot Castle Hotel
Tintagel PL34 0DQ
'phone: 01840 770202
website: www.camelotcastle.com/
email: enquiries@camelotcastle.com

6. BACKWAYS COVE

If you're visiting the popular beach known as Trebarwith Strand, a short walk south across the headland will bring you to Backways Cove. The cove is said to be haunted – but no one seems to know by what or by whom. It is thought possible that the ghosts are those of sailors who drowned when their ships were wrecked on the rocky coast. If you're passing this way, the answer is perhaps just to look and to listen for whatever might be there.

Backways Cove
Trebarwith Strand PL34 0HB

7. LAUNCESTON

A market town since Norman times, Launceston was the county town of Cornwall until 1835 when it was replaced by Bodmin. Part of the town wall is still standing, and the White Hart Hotel has a Norman doorway that may have originally belonged to the Friary at St Thomas. Two bridges cross the river Kensey, one dating from the mediaeval period and the other from 1580. The so-called New Bridge across the river Tamar was built in the early 16th century. Public executions took place on the castle green until the 19th century.

7a. Area near the Old Railway Station

A railway line no longer runs through here and the tracks have been removed, but the sound of a goods train passing through may sometimes be heard.

St Thomas Rd

Launceston PL15 8DA

7b. Higher Brown Quartils

If you leave Launceston on the B3254, heading south west, after about three miles you will come to the village of South Petherwin. In the late 1650s a young woman named Dorothy Dingley (or Dinglet) died there. Some versions of the story say that she was murdered, others that she died in childbirth, the father of her child being the son of a local farmer, one Mr Bligh. Some three years after her death Stephen Bligh, the farmer's younger son, started to see Dorothy's ghost when he was walking to school across a field known as Higher Brown Quartils. The local vicar, the Reverend John Ruddle, was called in. He walked the fields with Stephen, managed to talk to the ghost and, apparently, exorcised her. But there have been many reports of sightings since then, so it seems that Dorothy is still haunting the area.

The farm is now an abbattoir and is private property. However, the land is fairly flat so you can see a lot of the farm from the road. In addition to which, you may meet Dorothy walking along one of the roads surrounding the farm – a route she started to take when, in an attempt to avoid her, Stephen decided to walk to school along the road, rather than across the fields,.

South Petherwin
PL15 7JL

8. THE KING'S HEAD, FIVE LANES

This village of Five Lanes is said to have been inhabited since the time of the Norman Conquest but the King's Head was not built until 1623. During the Civil War it was, at different times, occupied by both Royalists and Parliamentarians. In the mid 18th century it became a staging post for coaches going to and from London. As a result, it acquired a somewhat shady reputation, with the local vicar commenting that it was frequented by smugglers and was a place where "shadowy deals" took place.

THE GHOSTS OF THE KING'S HEAD

If you're staying at the King's Head you may encounter Peggy Bray, a former landlady who walks around the building, making sure that the present incumbents are running the place to her satisfaction. Her footsteps are often heard at night on the first floor and some people are aware of a chill as they go past the door that is halfway along the corridor.

If you're keen to have a ghostly encounter, ask for room 3. Visitors staying in that room have heard tapping on the bedroom window and, in 2011, a paranormal investigation team heard a door latch being lifted and heavy footsteps (which were picked up by a recorder) .

The King's Head

5 Cross Lanes

Five Lanes, Altarnun PL15 7RX

'phone: 01566 86241

website: www.facebook.com/The-Kings-Head-Hotel-871709652898172/

The Kings Head serves food and has bed and breakfast facilities.

9. ROUGH TOR

Situated on Bodmin Moor at 1313 feet above sea level, Rough Tor (or Roughtor) is the second highest point in Cornwall, just 65 feet lower than the hill known as Brown Willy, which is also on Bodmin Moor. There are traces of Bronze Age occupation on the tor, and the remains of a large number of stone hut circles. In mediaeval times the tor was the site of a chapel dedicated to St Michael. This is the only known hill top chapel on Bodmin Moor and, most likely, was erected to serve travellers along the nearby ancient trackway. At the foot of Rough Tor there is a memorial to the men of the 43rd Wessex Division who were killed in World War II.

THE GHOST OF ROUGH TOR

The ghost is that of a servant girl, Charlotte Dymond who was murdered in 1844. At the time of her death, Charlotte was working for a woman called Phillippa Peter in the village of Penhale on the edge of Bodmin Moor. Two young men were courting Charlotte – twenty three year old Matthew Weekes, who worked for Mrs Peter, and Mrs Peter's nephew, 26 year old Thomas Prout. On the day that Charlotte died, she and Matthew went for a walk together – but Matthew returned alone and, when asked where Charlotte was, said he didn't know. The next morning, when she had still failed to return, Matthew said that he had walked with her as far as the gate in Higher Down Field and then she had gone onto the moor while he had walked to Halsworthy. By the following day, Mrs Peter was starting to accuse Matthew of killing Charlotte out of jealousy and, a few days later, several men from the village set off to search the moors.

Charlotte was found at the foot of Rough Tor with her throat cut. Her shoes, bonnet, bag, shawl and gloves were missing. Strangely, there was no blood – it looked as though she had been washed with water from a nearby stream. Matthew Weekes, who had by now gone to Plymouth where he had a sister, was arrested for the murder, found guilty and hanged at Bodmin, watched by about 20,000 people. However, there were many who believed that he was innocent, which may be the reason why Charlotte has been unable to rest. She haunts Rough Tor, wearing her Sunday gown and a silk bonnet. Your best chance of seeing her is on the anniversary of her death, 14th April, but the sound of footsteps and a feeling of someone being there are frequently reported at other times.

Rough Tor Car Park
Bodmin Moor PL32 9QJ

From the car park to Rough Tor itself is a walk of about a mile and a half.

10. BOLVENTOR

10a. Jamaica Inn

Bolventor, which lies just off the A30 in the middle of Bodmin Moor, is little more than a hamlet and owes its fame to the fact that it's the location of Jamaica Inn which was immortalised by Daphne du Maurier in her novel of the same name, published in 1936. Although there has been an inn on this site since 1547, the present building dates from 1750 and was an important coach stop on the turnpike road that ran between Bodmin and Launceston. Originally it was just known as The New Inn but the name was later changed, seemingly as a tribute to the Trelawney family who were important local landowners and two of whom served as Governors of Jamaica. At this time smuggling was rife in Cornwall, with much of the contraband being brought ashore at the north coast harbours of Boscastle, Trebarwith and Tintagel. In its isolated position in the middle of the moor, the inn was the perfect place for the illicit tea, brandy, lace and tobacco to be hidden until it could be distributed and sold further afield.

Over the years a number of renovations and additions were made, and the inn changed hands several times. Eventually, in 1880, it shed the last of its disreputable heritage and became a temperance hotel. During the Second

World War it once again became an inn and, in 1964, it was bought by the novelist Alistair Maclean, whose brother then ran it and developed it into a hotel. In 1973 it was sold again and many alterations and improvements were made. The Smugglers Museum, where you can see many artefacts and a film about Cornish smugglers and wreckers, was opened in 1998. There is also a Daphne du Maurier museum with exhibits that include letters written to the author by various members of the Royal family including the Queen. The inn last changed hands in 2014.

THE GHOSTS OF JAMAICA INN

A large number of ghosts can be seen or heard at Jamaica Inn. When television's Most Haunted team visited, they declared it to be one of the spookiest places they had ever investigated. And it's not just the older parts of the building – phantom figures have been seen in the newer parts too, including the gift shop.

Perhaps the ghost you're most likely to see is the man who sits silent and unmoving on the wall in front of the inn. He won't respond if you speak to him nor will he look at you as you walk past and he may disappear before your eyes. He is said to have been a sailor or a traveller and the story is that he was sitting at the bar drinking a tankard of ale when someone came through the door and asked him to come outside. He put down his tankard and did as he was asked – and next day his body was found on the moor. But who he was and why he was murdered (or by whom) is unknown. However, he is said to come back from time to time to finish his drink –

so at closing time on the night of the full moon the landlord leaves half a tankard of ale on the bar.

There is also a man who wears a three cornered hat and a cloak and who walks through closed doors. He is believed to have been a highwayman and you may be aware of a sudden drop in temperature when he appears. Sometimes he is seen in the reception area and occasionally he has appeared outside bedroom doors, holding a lantern.

If you stay overnight, the best rooms in which to experience something spooky are numbers 3, 4, 5, 6 and, in the new wing, 23. Room 3 is haunted by a woman with a crying baby - you may either see or hear them, or both. It's possible that she is Mary Downing who bore the landlord (who was married) an illegitimate son in 1834. A young boy of about 10 has also been seen in this room, a scratching noise has been heard in the walls and staff constantly find small fingerprints on the mirror.

In room 4 you are likely to experience strange smells (no, it's not the drains), and hear muffled voices (sometimes talking in a foreign language) or heavy footsteps. Guests have been known to wake in the night to find the highwayman (described above) standing by the bed near the window watching them.

Room 5 is said to be the room in which a little girl named Hannah stayed with her mother. The following day they boarded a ship which sank. You may hear footsteps or a rattling sound in the bathroom and you may even see small wet footprints on the carpet. If you're female, you may feel someone touching your legs when you're in bed. And if you have a child with you, be aware that any toys left out may be moved around. Also in room 5 is the 'mirror ghost', said to be the spectre of a child who is trapped behind the glass. Sometimes she appears with an anguished young woman who seems to be her mother. Whether she and Hannah are one and the same is not clear.

In room 6 guests have reported furniture being shaken, and an indistinct shape of a man has been seen in the doorway to the bathroom. If you're in room 23 and there's a knock at the door, you may open it to find a woman in Victorian clothes standing there!

No matter which room you're in, you may hear footsteps in the corridors during the night, particularly in the old building. You may also hear conversations in a foreign tongue in the restaurant or the stable bar. If it's a moonlit night, in the early hours of the morning there may be the sound of horses' hooves and the metal rims of carriage wheels in the courtyard outside. Some reports say that the wheels sound as though they're moving across gravel while others say they seem to be travelling over rough cobble stones.

And, as if all this wasn't enough, some people have seen the ghost of a man (thought to be a smuggler) walking around the courtyard in the middle of the night, while others have seen a young man sitting in the corner of the main bar or leaning against the fireplace. Children have been heard giggling in the kitchen and servery and a monk has been seen in the cellar and elsewhere. In the main bar, glasses have been known to smash for no reason and, in one of the bars, women have had their hair pulled.

Other apparitions include a man on horseback in the courtyard on foggy nights, a man hanging by his neck from a nearby tree, and a large semi-transparent dog running some twelve inches above the ground.

A young blonde woman in Victorian dress has been seen near the gift shop on what was once the path to the church but is now an internal corridor. She has also been seen in the shop itself, where things are often found scattered on the floor when the staff open in the morning. Nearby, in the men's toilet, unseen men may be heard arguing. And in the museum in the old stable block, look out for the ghost of a stable boy called David – and keep an eye on the model elephant in one of the cabinets, which sometimes moves of its own accord.

Jamaica Inn
Bolventor PL15 7TS
'phone: 01566 86250
website: www.jamaicainn.co.uk/
email: enquiry@jamaicainn.co.uk

The inn has a farm shop and a gift shop. Ghost Hunts and Murder Mystery evenings are held monthly.

10b. Road Between Bolventor and Five Lanes

Two different apparitions have been seen along this stretch of the A30. There is an old fashioned car containing four laughing men, which suddenly vanishes. And there is what seems to be a phantom hitch-hiker, who walks along the road near Jamaica Inn at night.

11. DOZMARY POOL

This stretch of water on Bodmin moor is not so much a pool as a lake, about a mile in circumference. It and its surrounding area have been designated a Site of Special Scientific Interest and lie within the Cornwall Area of Outstanding Natural Beauty,

The Pool has associations with the legend of King Arthur. It is said to be the place where Arthur rowed out to the Lady of the Lake and received the sword Excalibur from her. After the King was mortally wounded at the Battle of Camlann, Sir Bedivere took the sword and threw it back into the Pool, where it was caught by a woman's hand and held aloft before being taken down into the water.

The Pool is also associated with a ghost story.

THE GHOST OF DOZMARY POOL

Jan Tregeagle, who lived in the early 17th century, was a dishonest magistrate who used his position to acquire a fortune. Whether or not he was as evil as legend paints him it is impossible to say, but he certainly existed and it is said that he had to bribe the clergy to ensure that, after his death, his body would be buried in the consecrated ground of St Breock's churchyard. Presumably it was a large bribe, because legend has it that he murdered his wife and children and defrauded an orphan of an estate that was rightly his. One version of the legend says that he sold his soul to the devil.

The story that is best known nowadays is that, some time before he died, Tregeagle, acting as the lawyer for a local man, defrauded him over a piece of land. After Tregeagle's death, a dispute arose concerning this land and the case was taken to court. The two sides presented their arguments but, just as the judge was about to sum up, one of the claimants asked if he could call a final witness. Permission was granted and the name of Jan Tregeagle was called. To the astonishment of those present, Tregeagle's ghost materialised in the witness box. He was made to take the oath and admitted the fraud. As a result, the jury brought in a verdict in favour of the claimant.

There are various versions of what happened next. One says that the claimant, having won his case, ignored the judge's request to return the ghost to wherever he had come from. Another says that he was willing to do so but unable to. In these versions, the clergy was called in and, in an attempt to save Tregeagle's soul, set him the task of emptying Dozmary Pool (which at that time was thought to be bottomless) with a limpet shell. However, there is another version in which, after he had given his evidence in court, it was demons who refused to allow him to go back into his grave, and it was they who set him the task of draining the Pool. The demons, it is said, set a pack of phantom dogs to guard him and prevent his escape. One version of this says that he did, somehow, manage to escape but was then condemned either to weave ropes from the sand of Gwenor Cove or to sweep the sand from Porthcurno Cove to Mill Bay where he can be heard screaming whenever the incoming tide washes the sand back again.

A slightly different version of the story can be found in Miss M.A. Courtney's *Cornish Feasts and Folk-lore*, published in 1890:

Tregeagle ... was popularly supposed to have married and murdered many heiresses to obtain their money. One day, just before his death, he was present when one man lent a large sum to another without receiving receipt or security for it ... Soon after Tregeagle's death the borrower denied that he had ever had it, and the case was brought into Bodmin Court to be tried, when the defendant said, "If Tregeagle ever saw it I wish to God that Tregeagle may come into court and declare it." No sooner were the words spoken than Tregeagle appeared, and gave his witness in favour of the plaintiff, declaring "that he could not speak falsely; but he who had found it so easy to raise him would find it difficult to lay him." The money was paid, but the wretched man was followed night and day by the spirit, and great labour had the parsons and wise men before they could finally rid him of his tormentor.

Jan Tregeagle is said still to haunt the Pool. People hear him howling in despair, although this is thought to be more about the everlasting task he has been set rather than signifying any regret for his wicked deeds.

Dozmary Pool PL15 7TP

12. THE MANOR HOUSE INN, RILLA MILL

The village of Rilla Mill has been in existence since the mid 15th century. The inn was built in the 17th century and is said to be haunted by three ghosts. The commonest manifestations are disembodied footsteps and a sudden drop in temperature.

The Manor House Inn
Rilla Mill
Callington PL17 7NT
'phone: 01579 362354
website: www.manorhouserilla.co.uk/
email: contact@manorhouserilla.co.uk

The inn serves food and has a takeaway menu. It is wheelchair accessible and free WiFi is available.

13. THE CROW'S NEST INN, DARITE

The village of Darite owes its existence to the railway and to two mines – the Wheal Agar mine which was in the village itself and the South Caradon mine which was on the other side of the valley. By the late 1860s the mines were employing over 600 men between them.

The Crow's Nest is the oldest recorded building in the village, dating to the mid 17th century, and originally built as a house for a mine captain. After it became an inn, it was owned for a time by the captain of the nearby Glasgow mine who encouraged his employees to spend their earnings in the Crow's Nest. You can still see, attached to the outer wall of the inn, the bell that was rung to summon the miners to work.

THE GHOSTS OF THE CROW'S NEST INN

It is said that the inn has four ghosts, but the most well known of these (referred to as Eddie) is thought to be that of Edward Charles Murch, a landlord of the pub who, in the early 20th century, dropped dead behind the bar. And it seems that Eddie enjoys a bit of mischief – such as sweeping glasses off the bar and causing sudden drops in temperature. A former landlady, in the mid 20th century, said that she often heard the miners' bell ringing on winter mornings – but whether Eddie was responsible for that isn't known.

The inn also has a strange clock – although, once more, it's not possible to say whether Eddie has a hand in this. The clock is always 10 minutes fast. If it's put right in the evening, it will be 10 minutes fast again by the morning – and it never gains any more than this. If anyone tries to adjust it, in an attempt to get it to run normally, the clock jumps off the wall!

The Crow's Nest
Darite PL14 5JQ
'phone: 01579 345930
website: www.thecrowsnestcornwall.co.uk/
email: dan@thecrowsnestcornwall.co.uk

The inn serves food, is wheelchair accessible and has free WiFi available.

14. ST BARTHOLOMEW'S RECTORY, WARLEGGAN

In 1953 a road was built linking the A38 to the hamlet of Warleggan which, before this, was known as the most remote village in Cornwall. St Bartholomew's, the parish church, is part Norman and part 15th century in date.

THE GHOST OF ST BARTHOLOMEW'S RECTORY

The ghost is that of the Reverend Frederick W. Densham who was rector here between 1931 and 1953. He has been described by different writers as being autocratic, authoritarian, well meaning and eccentric. He was also deeply unpopular.

Densham was 61 when he arrived in Warleggan, having worked in Africa and in London's East End, but never before in a country parish. It didn't take long for him to alienate his new parishioners.

Shortly after taking office, Densham bought a litter of German shepherd puppies. Like all puppies, they grew rapidly and, uncontrolled by their owner, started to worry and even savage sheep in the surrounding fields. Naturally, this led to complaints from the local farmers. It is fair to say that

Densham over-reacted – he surrounded the rectory with an eight foot high fence of barbed wire. Since visitors could no longer approach the rectory to knock on the front door, he left an oil drum by the fence for people to bang on should they wish to see him.

He also angered the local people by closing the Sunday school and trying to change the times of the church services. He disliked organ music and, at one point, threatened to sell the church organ. To try to attract more people, he painted the inside of the church in garish colours but this had the opposite effect from the one he was hoping for. Eventually, he was left with no congregation at all, but he continued to hold services and give sermons to an empty church. Or not quite empty – he would put cards with the names of previous rectors on the front pews and preach to them!

Densham's father had been a Methodist minister and Densham still had an affinity with the Methodist church (indeed, no one seems to know why he chose to be ordained in the Church of England). He preached occasionally at the Methodist chapel in the village, extolling the benefits of vegetarianism and condemning whist drives and concerts, both of which he considered to be "amusements from hell". He endeared himself rather more to this congregation, however, and, after his death, was remembered for his kindness in sharing flowers from his garden and sending milk to those who were ill. He also built a playground for the children of the village.

Densham lived alone since he was unwilling to pay wages for staff, and slowly his house fell into disrepair. In 1953 the villagers, aware that no smoke had risen from the chimneys for a few days, broke in and found him dead. The only person to attend his funeral was his solicitor and his ashes were scattered not in the rectory garden as he wished but in Plymouth Garden of Remembrance.

Densham was the last rector of Warleggan. After his death the rectory was sold and converted into flats but he is still seen sometimes, walking along the path towards what was once his home.

The Church of St Bartholomew
Warleggan PL30 4HB

15. THE ST KEW INN, ST KEW

The earliest part of the inn (now the lounge bar) was built to house the stonemasons who, around the middle of the 15th century, came to St Kew to build the parish church dedicated to St James the Great. While they were living in the village, the stonemasons seem to have set up a brewery (most water at that time was undrinkable so everyone drank beer). It is possible that the brewery was in what is now the cellar of the inn, and it seems likely that the building was turned into an inn soon after the stonemasons left.

THE GHOST OF THE ST KEW INN

In the 1970s, during the course of some renovations, the skeleton of a teenage girl was discovered. Forensic dating suggested that she had been there for about 100 years but there was no evidence of who she was or why she had been buried there. Her body was reburied in consecrated ground and a slab was laid over the spot where she had been found. Since then, her ghost has appeared whenever any alterations are being made to the inn and she has become known as Adele. If you're there at a time when something in the inn has been changed, you may feel a drop in the temperature as she brushes past you or you may even see her, her eyes in a distant stare.

The St Kew Inn
St Kew PL30 3HB
'phone: 01208 841259
website: www.stkewinn.co.uk/

The inn serves food and has a large, pleasant garden.

16. WADEBRIDGE

Originally known as Wade, the town changed its name after the construction, in 1460, of a bridge across the River Camel. The bridge, which still stands, is 320 feet long and has 17 arches.

16a. The Molesworth Arms Hotel

The hotel dates from the 16th century, when it was a coaching inn.

THE GHOSTS OF THE MOLESWORTH ARMS

At midnight on New Year's Eve, a phantom coach and horses is driven into the hotel courtyard by a headless coachman. Some people see this apparation, some only hear the sound of the coach and horses while others just feel suddenly uncomfortable and apprehensive, even if they know nothing about the legend.

The Molesworth Arms Hotel
37 Molesworth Street
Wadebridge PL27 7DP (PL27 7QW to access car park)

'phone: 01208 812055

website: https://molesworthrarms.co.uk/

email: info@molesworthrarms.co.uk

The hotel offers pub food and has a restaurant.

16b. Trewornan Bridge

On nights when the moon is full, a phantom coach and horses has been seen crossing the 15th century bridge across the River Camel. The horses appear to be galloping at break-neck speed and disappear as soon as they reach the far side of the bridge. Whether this is the same coach that visits the Molesworth Arms is not clear.

16c. The Church of St Petroc, Egloshayle

Egloshayle was once a village in its own right but over the years it has become part of Wadebridge as the town has expanded.

Two ghosts haunt St Petroc's churchyard and, for a chance to see one or both of them, you need to visit at full moon. The first ghost is a phantom rabbit that runs across the churchyard and disappears into the boundary wall. And the second is a man who died as a result of an accident with a shotgun when he was trying to shoot the rabbit!

The Church of St Petroc

Egloshayle PL27 6AD

17. LITTLE PETHERICK

The village of Little Petherick straddles the A389 Wadebridge to Padstow road. If you are on this road during the summer months, close to the Rosehill holiday cottages, you may see what seems to be a short man (or perhaps woman) lying on the road, apparently scrabbling at the surface. One person who got a good look at the apparition reported that it has no face.

Little Petherick PL27 7QT

18. PADSTOW

Padstow has been a busy fishing port and a centre of boat building since Tudor times. It retains two ancient seasonal customs – the Obby Oss (or Hobby Horse) festival on May Day and Mummers Days on Boxing Day and New Year's Day. The first consists of two separate processions around the town, led by a Hobby Horse, accompanied by singing and music from accordions, melodeons and drums. The second also involves singing and dancing, with those taking part wearing masks or painting their faces black.

18a. The Beach to the North of the Town

People standing on the beach after sunset, have heard the sound of oars passing through the water although there is no boat in sight.

18b. Caffe Rojano

The restaurant opened in 1974 but the building dates back to the 18th century. A former, deceased owner of the property is still around and, in the past, has been quite active – on one occasion he threw a barrel down the staircase.

Caffe Rojano
9 Mill Square
Padstow PL28 8AE
'phone: 01841 532093
website: www.paul-ainsworth.co.uk/cafferojano/about/

The restaurant specialises in Italian cuisine. Free WiFi is available.

18c. St Petroc's

The building was once the home of a young woman named Annie Rawlings who, when it seemed that she was going to be evicted, committed suicide. She remains devoted to the building and is said to haunt it to this day.

St Petroc's
New Street
Padstow PL28 8EA
'phone: 01841 532700
website: www.rickstein.com/restaurants/
st-petrocs-bistro/

The restaurant is run by Rick Stein. Free WiFi is available.

18d. Prideaux Place

This manor house was built in 1592 and has been the home of the Prideaux-Brune family ever since. The family history, however, goes back much further than that – the Prideaux are recorded as having been Lords of the Manor at Prideaux Castle, Luxulyan (near Lostwithiel) in Norman times. Prideaux Place was used as a base for American servicemen during World War Two

THE GHOSTS OF PRIDEAUX PLACE

In the kitchen you may see a scullery boy running round the room and a small child going into the pantry (but not coming out again).

On the main staircase people have reported seeing two female apparitions, one wearing green and the other grey. The lady in green has also been seen in the drawing room, the great chamber, the wooded area in the garden and a nearby cave. She is thought to be the ghost of Honor Fortescue, the wife of Humphrey Prideaux, who threw herself off a balcony after her husband died. She has, on occasion, been known to chase people out of the bedrooms.

In the morning room look out for a woman in 19th century clothes who sits in a corner sewing. In addition, there is a dog that roams round the building and is often seen standing and growling by the bed in the Park Room, a guest bedroom whose atmosphere some people find very oppressive.

Prideaux Place

Padstow PL28 8RP

'phone: 01841 532411

website: https://prideauxplace.co.uk/

email: office@prideauxplace.co.uk

In recent years the house has been extensively restored. There are 81 rooms in total and the owners offer guided tours of some of the best of these. There are also gardens, a deer park and a café.

19. BEDRUTHAN STEPS

Bedruthan lies just off the B3276 between Newquay and Padstow. People who walk along the cliffs at night have seen indistinct 'grey forms' – possibly the ghosts of miners who used to work in the area – and some have reported hearing the tramp of their heavy boots and the sound of their tools.

Bedruthan Steps
Bedruthan PL27 7UW

20. BODMIN JAIL

Bodmin Jail was built in the 1770s by Napoleonic prisoners of war and, at the time, was considered to be the latest thing in prison design. It was based on plans advocated by the prison reformer John Howard (after whom the Howard League for Penal Reform is named) and was innovative in that prisoners were put in individual cells, men and women were segregated, and there were separate areas of the building to house felons, 'misdemeanants' and debtors. But life was not easy for inmates – prisoners were subjected to hard labour and between 1785 and 1909 fifty five people, including eight women, were executed by hanging. Public hangings took place until 1862 and thousands of people would come to watch.

For the first twenty years or so of its existence, the number of inmates was fairly low, but by 1820 all the cells had more than one occupant. To try to cope with the chronic overcrowding, several extensions were built during the 19th century.

In 1911 the women's section was closed and the remaining female prisoners were transferred to Plymouth. The number of male prisoners declined, with the last one leaving in 1916. The jail was officially decommissioned in 1927.

In 1930 the building was turned into a casino and night-club but it started to deteriorate after a section of the roof had to be removed for repairs and the walls began to crumble. Much of it remained derelict until 2004 when it was bought by a local family who restored parts of it in order to turn it into a tourist attraction. In 2015 a major redevelopment began, including the construction of a 70 bed hotel within the building.

THE GHOST OF SELINA WADGE

Selina was arrested in 1878 for the murder of her two year old disabled son, Harry. She told the police that her lover, James Westwood, had urged her to murder Harry, saying that he would marry her if she did so. However, Westwood vigorously denied this.

Selina was tried and found guilty, although the jury recommended leniency because they said that the murder was not premeditated and Selina had taken good care of her other children. But the judge disagreed and sentenced her to be hanged.

On 15th August 1878 she stood on the scaffold moments before her execution, clutching a white handkerchief and said "Lord deliver me from this miserable world". Her body was left dangling for an hour before being taken down for burial in the prison grounds.

When seen, Selina's ghost is still holding the handkerchief. She often approaches small children who have been known to ask their parents about the crying lady in the long dress.

And some pregnant women have become very emotional on the third floor of the prison, affected by her presence.

THE GHOST OF CHARLOTTE DYMOND

It seems that ghosts can appear in two places at the same time. Charlotte Dymond, whose story was told in the section on Rough Tor (no. 9) has been seen on April 14th, the anniversary of her death, both there and in Bodmin Jail. Her association with the jail is that Matthew Weekes, who was arrested for her murder, was hanged here in August 1844, with some 20,000 people watching. In recent years, doubt has been cast on whether in fact he was guilty and it may be for this reason that Charlotte haunts the prison dressed, as at Rough Tor, in her Sunday best and wearing a silk bonnet.

OTHER PARANORMAL HAPPENINGS AT THE JAIL

Many visitors report a feeling of desolation and despair, which is hardly surprising. Screams, footsteps and disembodied voices have been heard around the building, as well as the rattling of keys. Doors have been slammed and stones and other objects thrown by invisible hands. One ghost hunting group picked up strange grunting sounds on a tape they had set to record through the night.

The ghost of William Hampton, who was hanged for murder, has been seen, and the figure of a priest has appeared in what used to be the chapel.

Also be prepared for orbs, strange shadows and sudden drops in temperature.

Bodmin Jail
Berrycoombe Rd
Bodmin PL31 2NR
'phone: 01208 76292
website: www.bodminjail.org/
email: info@bodminjail.org

As well as regular tours of the jail, there is a Bodmin Jail After Dark Experience which is described as "an all night paranormal journey" consisting of a two hour tour after which the lights go out and those present have the opportunity to use a variety of techniques to experience the paranormal. Bodmin Jail also has a resident medium who runs two events each month. The whole site has disabled access.

21. LANHYDROCK

This Grade I listed house was built in the 1630s by Sir Richard Robartes on the site of a farm owned by the priory of St Petroc. It remained in the Robartes family until 1953 when it was given to the National Trust. In 1881 a devastating fire destroyed most of the building – only the north wing, entrance porch and gatehouse remained. Lady Robartes, who was 68 at the time, was rescued from an upstairs room but died a few days later. Her husband died the following year and the rebuilding of the house was carried out by their son, Thomas, who also undertook the restoration of the adjacent church.

THE GHOSTS OF LANHYDROCK

Lanhydrock boasts numerous ghosts. A small elderly woman dressed in grey, seen in the long gallery and drawing room, is thought to be the ghost of the Lady Robartes who died as a result of the fire. Those who see her are unaware that she is a ghost until they approach her – at which point she disappears.

A man who was hanged outside the gatehouse by Royalists during the Civil War sometimes puts in an appearance, as does a ghost described as "a dapper gent wearing Victorian clothes and a top hat". Three servants still haunt their former workplace – Albert Leah who was head butler and died around 1890, Annabelle O'Connor who committed suicide at the age of 22, and a footman whose job it was to clean the shoes.

At least four children have been seen around the house – Emily who died in the 1760s aged 10, a little boy called Robert who haunts the luggage room, a nameless teenage boy who was trampled to death by a horse in 1795, and a toddler who died from scarlet fever in the 1820s. And in addition to all of these there is a Catholic priest who has been around since the 16th century because, so it is said, he is weighed down by guilt after having an affair with a servant girl.

Visitors often smell cigar smoke or strong perfume as they walk round the house and are aware of sudden drops in temperature. A team of psychic investigators reported hearing what sounded like a heavy piece of furniture being dragged across a wooden floor and a young girl giggling in the nursery suite. People have also been aware of ghostly presences in the servants' quarters and the prayer room, lights have been seen moving around the long gallery, objects have moved around by themselves and unexplained moving shadows have been seen on the teak staircase. Photographs taken in the house may show orbs – although it's not unknown for visitors' cameras suddenly to stop working.

Lanhydrock
Bodmin PL30 4AB

'phone: 01208265950

website: www.nationaltrust.org.uk/lanhydrock

email: lanhydrock@nationaltrust.org.uk

The house has fifty rooms, furnished in the high Victorian style. There are 450 acres of park and woodland as well as colourful herbaceous borders and a formal parterre. The estate can be explored on cycle trails and bicycles are available for hire.

A tour of the house involves several steps and ramps. Manual wheelchairs and a countryside mobility tramper are available for loan, and there are accessible toilets.

22. BRADDOCK DOWN

A battle fought in January 1643 between the Royalist and the Parliamentarian forces became known as the Battle of Braddock Down. It was an important battle in the Civil War, as it secured Cornwall for the King. Fifteen hundred Parliamentarians were captured and 200 killed, whereas the Royalists sustained only a few losses. The exact location of the battle is uncertain but it was either within Boconnoc Park or a mile or two further north, near the village of Braddock. It is said that if you visit the area on January 19th, the anniversary of the battle, you can hear the thunder of hooves as the two sides ride into the fray.

23. THE WEARY FRIAR INN, PILLATON

Originally built in the 12th century to house the monks of the church of St Odulphus (which is to be found a few yards to the east, along a narrow lane) the building later became a coaching inn.

THE GHOST OF THE WEARY FRIAR INN

Although there don't seem to be any written reports of haunting in the pub in the last few years, it is more than likely that the ghost is still there, especially as he takes the form of a monk and so, presumably, has been around for many centuries. The monk has been seen on the staircase and, in addition, ornaments have been seen to move by themselves. Some visitors have reported hearing a clock ticking loudly – although there is no clock.

The Weary Friar Inn
Pillaton PL12 6QS
'phone: 01579 350238
website: www.wearyfriar.co.uk/en-GB

email: info@wearyfriar.co.uk

The pub has three bed and breakfast rooms and a self-contained holiday cottage. It serves food and is wheelchair accessible. Free WiFi is available.

24. COTEHELE

Mainly built between 1485 and 1687 but with parts dating to the 1300s, Cotehele was the home of the Edgcumbe family for centuries and is now owned by the National Trust. It is a Grade II listed building.

THE GHOSTS OF COTEHELE

The ghost who is seen most frequently is a girl with long hair, dressed all in white. She appears so normal and solid that many people who encounter her are not aware that she's a ghost.

Some visitors have heard plaintive music or smelled a herbal fragrance and have seen misty figures around the house. Figures on horseback have been seen outside the house and a robed figure has been spotted standing by the front door.

Some people find that the King Charles Room, where Charles I is said to have slept, has an unpleasant atmosphere.

Cotehele
Saltash PL12 6TA
'phone: 01579 351346

website: www.nationaltrust.org.uk/cotehele

email: cotehele@nationaltrust.org.uk

25. CALSTOCK

There were people living in Calstock in Roman times and, from the 5th century, it was a port and probably a mining town. By the 19th century it had a population of 7000, with copper, tin, silver and tungsten being mined here and shipped from the quay. A decline in mining led to a decline in the industrial importance of the town in the early 20th century. The railway viaduct carrying the Tamar Valley Railway, which runs between Plymouth and Gunnislake, was built in 1907 and is 120 feet high with twelve 60 foot arches.

25a. The Road Leading to Calstock

A group of miners, carrying candles and wearing their traditional clothes, are said to have been seen a number of times on "the road leading to Calstock". Which road is meant is unclear but it may well be Eric Road, a narrow track that runs alongside the railway line, since this is probably the route the miners would have taken when going to and fro between the town and the mine, which was located above the bend in the River Tamar.

25b. The Boot Inn

Dating back to 1662, the inn is in the centre of the village.

THE GHOSTS OF THE BOOT INN

Various paranormal activities have been reported such as loud bangs, lights going on and off and the sound of bottles being banged together. Some people have reported feeling as though someone has touched or prodded them. A black figure has been seen in the function room and on one occasion the landlord was unable to shut a door because of an unseen 'someone' pushing against it.

The Boot Inn
Fore Street
Calstock PL18 9RN
'phone: 01822 834866
website: www.facebook.com/TheBootInn25/
email: thebootinn25@gmail.com

The inn serves food. Free WiFi is available.

26. PORT ELIOT MANOR HOUSE, ST GERMANS

The manor house is believed to be the oldest continually inhabited house in the UK, having been lived in for over 1000 years, but Port Eliot itself is even older. In the mid 10th century there was an Augustinian monastery here, and a 1500 year old glazed tiled floor gives evidence of late Iron Age occupation. The house was remodelled in the 18th century by Sir John Soane, while the gardens and park are the creation of Humphrey Repton. The house is Grade I listed.

THE GHOST OF PORT ELIOT MANOR HOUSE

The ghost of a monk has been seen in the house. He is described as harmless and sad-looking and tends to be seen mainly by children (he once gatecrashed a party, causing it to be ended prematurely).

Port Eliot Manor House
St Germans PL12 5ND
website: www.porteliot.co.uk/
email: info@porteliot.co.uk

There are holiday lets on the Port Eliot estate, available through AirB&B.

27. THE FINNYGOOK INN, CRAFTHOLE

The inn dates from the 15th century but had to be refurbished extensively in 2017 after being badly damaged by fire. It is known to have been a haunt of smugglers and criminals during the 18th century.

THE GHOST OF THE FINNYGOOK INN

One of the smugglers who frequented the inn was a certain Silas Finney who was murdered at Bliger's Well, a hill between Crafthole and Portwrinkle, after he got into an argument over a consignment of smuggled goods. One version of the story says that his body was concealed in a well lying below the present kitchen of the inn. But, whatever his ultimate fate, Silas continues to haunt the inn and some people claim also to have seen him on the hill where he was killed.

The Finnygook Inn
Cliff Road
Crafthole PL11 3BQ

'phone: 01503 230338

website: www.facebook.com/finnygook

email: eat@finnygook.co.uk

The inn has a restaurant. It is wheelchair accessible and free WiFi is available.

28. THE JOLLY SAILOR INN, LOOE

The inn dates back to the early 16th century, while the main beam in the bar is said to have originally been part of a ship that fought at the Battle of Trafalgar – either HMS Indefatigable or a French ship that was captured. Whatever its provenance, when the ship was broken up in 1815 the landlord of the Jolly Sailor made sure that the beam found its way to his inn. Some of the other beams are said to have been from the ships in the Spanish Armada which were shipwrecked off Looe in 1588.

THE GHOSTS OF THE JOLLY SAILOR INN

A coachman, with his hair tied back and wearing a frock coat, ruffled shirt and leather gaiters tends to materialise and then disappear again. A young girl has been seen walking through the walls on the landing and a small lady dressed in what has been described as "old fashioned dress" has chatted to staff and visitors before disappearing into the nearest wall. There have also been reports of a ghostly white rabbit!

The Jolly Sailor Inn
Princes Square
Looe PL13 2EP
'phone: 01503 263387
website: www.jollysailorlooe.co.uk/

The inn offers bed and breakfast and pub food. Free WiFi is available.

29. POLPERRO

Like many other Cornish fishing villages, Polperro was a haunt of smugglers during the 18th century.

For much of the 19th century pilchard fishing was the main industry here, with the fish being processed and packed in factories built close to the harbour. Boat building was also a major industry for many years.

29a. Willy Willock's Hole

Despite its name, this is actually a cave system and the ghost, according to one version, is said to be that of a local fisherman who died after getting lost while exploring the system. Another version says that he was a smuggler who went into the caves to hide from the Customs men and drowned when the tide came in. Whichever version you believe, on stormy nights he can still be heard calling for help.

In recent times, a holidaymaker, looking at some photos that he'd taken in the caves, was surprised to see that a ghostly figure was visible in the background. So it seems that it may be possible to see Willy Willock as well as hear him.

29b. The Three Pilchards Inn

The inn was originally built in the 16th century but its name is thought to have been bestowed at a later date and to relate to the three pilchard factories that were in the village. In the 19th century, one of its landlords, Charles Joliff, was a notorious smuggler who would announce a newly arrived shipment of contraband to his accomplices by leaving a saddled horse outside the inn.

THE GHOSTS OF THE THREE PILCHARDS

At some time in the late 19th century, a landlord who was a heavy drinker and had a violent temper beat his wife to death. Their teenage son tried to defend his mother and he, too, was killed. Every now and again the sounds of the struggle, together with the wife's screams, are heard coming from the second floor of the inn. And the ghosts of the woman and her son have been seen, briefly, standing at the top of the stairs, then fading away leaving a sense of overwhelming sadness.

A happier ghost is the woman who has frequently been seen in the back yard, milking a phantom cow. But she, too, is said to appear and disappear very quickly. There is also an elderly woman who haunts the upstairs part of the inn and a cheerful old man who appears near the end of the bar, smiles and nods at anyone who notices him – and then vanishes. But even if you're not fortunate enough to see one of these in their brief visits to the inn, you may well smell violets in the bar. The scent is said to be quite strong and to come and go.

The Three Pilchards
Quay Road
Polperro PL13 2QZ
'phone: 01503 272233
website: www.threepilchardspolperro.co.uk/
email: thethreepilchards@hotmail/com

The inn serves food, and free WiFi is available.

29c. The Crumplehorn Inn

The building, which originated as a counting house and mill in Elizabethan times, has only been an inn since 1972. The hamlet of Crumplehorn, whose origins are recorded in the Domesday Book, has had several different variations of its name – Temylhorne and then Termblehorn in the late 16th century, Cremblehorn in the early 18th century, and Crumple Horn from the early 19th century.

THE GHOSTS OF THE CRUMPLEHORN INN

The inn is said to be haunted by Zephaniah Job who died in 1822. Nicknamed 'The Smugglers' Banker,' he both organised and financed smuggling into Polperro. People have reported glimpsing 'something' in the bar but when they turn to see what it is, it has disappeared.

Whispering voices have been heard by a number of people late at night and are thought to be those of a young World

War I soldier and his girlfriend. The story is that he deserted and hid in the loft of the inn but was found and sent back, where he was killed in the trenches.

And it's not only the bar and the loft that are the sites of paranormal activity – there seems to be quite a lot in the toilets too, with doors opening and shutting by themselves!

The Crumplehorn Inn & Mill
Polperro PL13 2RJ
'phone: 01503 272348
website: https://thecrumplehorninn.co.uk/
email: reception@thecrumplehorninn.co.uk

The inn has bed and breakfast and self catering accommodation and serves food. It is wheelchair accessible and free WiFi is available.

30. FOWEY

Local legend says that Jesus visited Fowey when he was a child, brought here by Joseph of Arimathea who was visiting the local tin mines. A cross, known as 'Punches Cross', was erected by the monks at Tywardreath, to commemorate this – it still stands below the cliffs, south west of St Saviour's Point. Whether or not the legend is true, there has been a church in Fowey since the 7th century.

The estuary of the River Fowey forms a natural harbour and the town was once an important centre for both trade and piracy.

30a. The Footpath to Readymoney Cove

People walking along the footpath that runs between Readymoney Cove and the top of the town, have reported seeing the ghost of a soldier returning home after the First World War.

30b. The Safe Harbour Hotel

Previously known as the Commercial Inn, this is an old coaching inn a few minutes' walk from the harbour.

THE GHOSTS OF THE SAFE HARBOUR HOTEL

The ghosts here have no specific names or histories, but visitors to the hotel have reported seeing 'ghostly shapes'.

The Safe Harbour Hotel
58 Lostwithiel Street
Fowey PL23 1BQ
'phone: 01726 833379
website: www.staustellbrewery.co.uk/pub/fowey/safe-harbour-hotel

The hotel is wheelchair accessible and free WiFi is available.

30b. The Ship Inn

This is one of the oldest buildings in Fowey. Although English Heritage believes that it was built as a merchant's house in the 15th century, traditionally it is said to have been built in 1570 for John Rashleigh, who was related to both Francis Drake and Walter Raleigh. Like them, John was a sailor, visiting the Americas and taking part in the defeat of the Spanish Armada before returning to Fowey to become the town's Member of Parliament.

THE GHOSTS OF THE SHIP INN

The inn is haunted by a woman known as Alice, who sometimes has a dog with her. She has been seen around the inn but, at other times, just her footsteps are heard.

The Ship Inn
Trafalgar Square
Fowey PL23 1AZ
'phone: 01726 832230
website: https://shipfowey.co.uk
email: eat@shipfowey.co.uk

The inn's website describes it as being "a beautiful, higgledy-piggeldy old building with nooks and crannies and old panelled rooms at every turn". Bed and breakfast is available, as is free WiFi.

31. THE CHURCH OF ST ANDREW, TYWARDREATH

Tywardreath, like Fowey, has associations with a member of the Rashleigh family. This Rashleigh, however, was of a much later generation than John and even spelled his name differently. He was William Rashley and, like his ancestor, he was Member of Parliament for Fowey. His life has been commemorated by a plaque in St Andrew's, the parish church.

THE GHOSTS OF THE CHURCH OF ST ANDREW

William Rashley died in 1855 and, on the anniversary of his death – May 14th – strange things have been observed in and around the church. What appears at first to be black smoke has been seen coming out of William's memorial plaque and then taking human shape before drifting round the church. At the same time, loud bangs have been heard and, on one occasion, a wall-hanging suddenly fell to the floor. On occasion, the church bells have rung of their own accord – something that may or may not be associated with William Rashley. In addition, the figure of a monk has been seen standing in the church.

The Church of St Andrew
Tywardreath PL24 2QQ

32. THE ST AUSTELL BREWERY, ST AUSTELL

This is the oldest independent family brewery in Cornwall and it has stood on the same site since 1893. There is an interactive museum telling the story of local pubs, wines and spirits and their Cornish creators, and you can take a guided tour of the brewery. Listen out for disembodied footsteps coming down the stairs – they are said to be those of the ghost of the founder of the brewery, Walter Hicks. You may also get a whiff of his cigar smoke.

The St Austell Brewery
63 Trevarthian Road
St Austell PL25 4BY
'phone: 01726 66022
website: www.staustellbreweryvisitorcentre.co.uk/
email: vcoffice@staustellbrewery.co.uk

33. THE QUAKER BURIAL GROUND, ST MEWAN

If you travel along the A390 from St. Austell towards St. Mewan, just before you get to the 40mph sign you will see a large field on your left. This is the site of the old Quaker Burial Ground. When the new road was built in the 1960s, the headstones were removed and the burial ground was covered over with the excavated earth. But on a still evening it is said that you may see some oddly moving mist – the ghostly remains of those who were buried there.

34. THE LOST GARDENS OF HELIGAN

Since the 16th century, the Heligan estate has been owned by the Tremayne family and their descendants. During the 19th century, four generations of Tremaynes created magnificent gardens which included many exotic plants. At the start of the First World War there were 22 gardeners employed to care for the gardens. But by 1916 there were only eight, the rest having gone to fight – and many to be killed – in the trenches. After the war, the owner moved to Italy and rented out the house and estate. And this was how it remained. During World War II the house was used by the United States Army. And then, in the 1970s, the house – but not the gardens – was sold. And, extraordinarily, the gardens seem just to have been forgotten about.

In 1990, a descendant of the Tremayne family, John Willis, exploring the jungle that the gardens had become, was surprised to find a small building overgrown with vines. His curiosity was piqued and he resolved to try to restore the gardens to what they once had been. But it would be a mammoth task. Interviewed by Enchanted Living magazine, Heligan's marketing manager spoke of brambles over twenty feet high invading the derelict greenhouses, and the melon yard made almost impassable by self-seeded trees. Amazingly, some original features and historic plants remained.

After decades of hard work, the gardens have been restored and now boast themed gardens, a crystal grotto, an Italian garden and the only extant functional pineapple pit in Europe.

THE GHOSTS OF THE LOST GARDENS OF HELIGAN

The most haunted areas seem to be the rockery, the fruit store and the melon garden, with its little cottage. Some of the gardeners prefer to work in pairs in these areas which, they say, make them feel uneasy. In the melon house, seeds have been moved around and the lids of forcing pots have been seen to be lifted by unseen hands.

People have spoken of seeing black shapes darting around and "sinister presences" in the grotto, and figures have been seen standing round the wishing well while, in the wooded ravine known as the 'Lost Valley', one of the people helping to restore the gardens saw a huge black shape rising up before disappearing into the trees. A pentacle was later found in the grounds arousing suspicions that Satanic rituals might have taken place here.

Another ghost, the Grey Lady, is often seen walking along the path from the house before vanishing among the trees. Many people feel as though they are being watched as they walk round the gardens but, despite this, many find the gardens peaceful and inspirational.

The Lost Gardens of Heligan

Pentewan

St.Austell PL26 6EN

'phone: 01726 845100

website: www.heligan.com/

35. THE CROWN INN, ST EWE

The inn, which was built in the 16th century, is said to be haunted by a previous landlord, Norman Jeffery. No one has ever seen him directly – just a shadowy shape is observed – but there have been reports of sudden drops in temperature (particularly at the table nearest the fireplace) and his image has been detected on film. In one shot he is with a dog who is also a regular visitor and seems to make himself felt when customers bring their dogs into the bar.

The Crown Inn
Churchtown
St Ewe PL26 6EY
'phone: 01726 843322
website: www.staustellbrewery.co.uk/pub/st-ewe/crown-inn

The inn serves food and is wheelchair accessible. Free WiFi is available.

36. THE CHURCH OF ST LADOCA , LADOCK

Originally a Saxon church, most of St Ladoca's was rebuilt in the 19th century and it is now a Grade I listed building.

If you visit the church, you may catch a glimpse of a ghostly figure out of the corner of your eye, but it will quickly disappear. It seems that your chances of seeing it are higher when the church bells are being rung.

The Church of St Ladoca
Ladock TR2 4PL

37. ROCHE CHAPEL, ROCHE

This 15th century ruined chapel stands on a rugged outcrop of rock on the outskirts of Roche village. Dedicated to St Michael, it is said once to have been inhabited by a hermit and his daughter. Legend also has it that ill-fated lovers Tristan and Isolde hid here from King Mark, to whom Isolde was promised in marriage. To visit it, you need a head for heights as it is only accessible via a 66 foot ladder hammered into the rock.

THE GHOSTS OF ROCHE CHAPEL

The chapel is said to be haunted by a miner (or a smuggler) who was murdered nearby. It is also said that the ghost of Jan Tregeagle tried to find refuge in the chapel or was banished here after he failed to empty Dozmary Pool (see section 11 above) and that he now haunts the rock, especially when there is a high wind. A phantom monk has also been seen.

Roche Chapel
Roche Rock, Roche PL26 8FG

38. CASTLE AN DINAS, ST COLUMB MAJOR

Situated to the north of Goss Moor, this huge hillfort is reputed to have been one of the bases used by King Arthur, although it actually originates from the 2nd or 3rd century BCE. Cornish legends say it is where Cador, Duke of Cornwall (the husband of Arthur's mother) died.

THE GHOSTS OF CASTLE AN DINAS

Some people have seen ghostly armies (said to be those of King Arthur) and heard the sounds of battle at Castle Dinas but there is another solitary ghost who is sometimes encountered here. In 1671 a man called John Trehenban murdered two local girls and was sentenced to be locked in a cage on the summit of Castle an Dinas until he starved to death. The sounds of him rattling the chains that held him may still be heard. Some visitors to the hillfort have strong reactions to its energies, feeling dizzy or faint or experiencing pains in their heads when they stand on the summit.

Castle an Dinas, St Columb Major TR9 6JB

39. TRERICE, KESTLE MILL

Trerice was built in 1573 by Sir John Arundell on the site of a 14th century house, parts of which are still standing. Sir John's father – also called Sir John Arundell – had made a fortune in the service of Henry VIII and the house stayed in the family for nearly 250 years. During the Civil War it was seized by Cromwell (because the Arundells supported the Royalist cause) and then returned after the Restoration of the Monarchy in 1660. In 1802 it was taken over by the Acland family who stayed there until 1915 when the house was sold. In 1953 it was acquired by the National Trust.

THE GHOSTS OF TRERICE

The most commonly encountered ghost is that of a young servant girl. The story goes that the Lord Arundell of her time led a life of debauchery and made her pregnant. Depending on which version you believe, she committed suicide when he discarded her, died in childbirth or was killed on his orders. She makes her presence known by a sudden drop in temperature or the rustling of her skirts. Her presence seems strongest in the library and it has been suggested that this was the room in which she died. Various unexplained noises throughout the house tend to be attributed to her. She is usually accompanied by a scent of lilac, as is the Grey Lady who walks along the gallery in the north wing and then down the stone steps. Some people think that the servant girl and the Grey Lady are one and the same person. In the 1980s builders who were carrying out repairs in the house heard the sound of long skirts swishing along the floor and saw doors opening and closing by themselves.

Two ghosts are associated with the courtyard. The first is a stable boy who is said to have been killed when the horses he was tending suddenly bolted and trampled him to death. The other is a headless rider who, at midnight on moonlit nights, rides across the courtyard with his head under his arm.

Trerice

Kestle Mill TR8 4PG

'phone: 01637875404

website: www.nationaltrust.org.uk/trerice

email: trerice@nationaltrust.org.uk

The house is described as having fine interiors and a delightful garden.

40. NEWQUAY

Originally a small fishing port, Newquay acquired its current name in the 15th century when a new harbour was built. Pilchard fishing was the main industry of the town for many years.

40a. Area Between Towan Beach and Belushi's Pub

People walking along this short stretch of coastline sometimes hear a woman crying or see a misty floating figure. It's said to be the ghost of a woman who died in the 1930s when an old smugglers' tunnel collapsed while she was exploring it.

Towan Beach
Newquay TR7 1DU

Belushi's Pub
35 Fore Street
Newquay TR7 1HD

40b. The Gannel

While not haunted by a specific ghost, this tidal estuary has been the site of a particular paranormal experience over many years. People hear dreadful screams which seem to be coming from the river itself. An unidentified 19th century writer described it as "a thousand voices pent up in misery, with one long wail dying away in the distance". Some say that it is the cry of a legendary bird or a troubled spirit known as the Gannel Crake.

The Gannel
Newquay TR7 2AW

40c. Barrowfields

There were originally 15 barrows or tumuli here but few remain. When one was excavated, it revealed the remains of a Bronze Age chieftain, buried here some 3500 years ago.

The sound of galloping horses has been heard when the moon is new, and a headless horseman, who rides several feet above the present ground level, has been seen.

Barrowfields
Newquay TR7 2PQ

40d. Newquay Golf Club

The club was established in 1890. The club house, which was bought in 1906, was originally a mansion called The Tower and was built for the Molesworth family in 1835.

THE GHOSTS OF NEWQUAY GOLF CLUB

If you're a golfer and decide to have a round of golf here, don't leave before checking out the bar and the snooker room! Even though smoking in public places has been banned since 2007, the smell of smoke is evident in the bar. A previous owner of the house has also been seen in the bar. And there is a ghostly elderly man who sits quietly in a corner of the snooker room.

Newquay Golf Club
Tower Road
Newquay TR7 1LT
'phone: 01637 874354
website: www.newquaygolfclub.co.uk/
email: info@newquaygolfclub.co.uk

Visitors are welcome to play the course.

40e. The Harbour

One evening in 2009, an empty boat was found close to the

harbour. This was reported to the harbourmaster who identified it as a boat that had been lost at sea 18 years before. But before anyone could investigate the boat, it had disappeared. Whether this was an isolated sighting is unclear, but if you're by the harbour during the evening and see a strange boat that appears to be unmanned, this may be it!

40f. The Headland Hotel

The hotel, which was built in 1900, is a Grade II listed building. The site itself is designated a Site of Special Scientific Interest because of the numerous fossils that have been found in the grounds.

If you've seen the movie of Roald Dahl's *The Witches,* you may well recognise it as the 'Hotel Excelsior'. The bedrooms used for filming were numbers 205, 223 and 227. At Halloween every year the hotel holds a 'spooky afternoon tea tribute'.

THE GHOSTS OF THE HEADLAND HOTEL

If you happen to be in the hotel basement at 2am on a Sunday morning, you may hear a bell ringing to summon a servant – although all the bells are disconnected. The ghost of a little girl has been seen running around the hotel.

During World War II, the hotel served as an RAF hospital and, late at night, ghostly men in uniform have been seen walking along the corridors. Some people have heard the voices of the wounded crying out in pain, and nurses have been seen as well, wearing capes and frilly caps. One of these nurses has been seen walking through a wall where there used to be a door into the Ladies, while others have walked through closed doors into bedrooms. Some guests have been woken by a nurse stroking their faces.

The Headland Hotel
Fistral Beach
Headland Road, Newquay TR7 1EW
'phone: 01637 872211
website: www.headlandhotel.co.uk/
email: reception@headlandhotel.co.uk

40g. Old Headland Area

If you're in Newquay a week or two before Christmas, you may see a floating light moving along the path in the Fistral area before disappearing near the old lifeguard station. It is said to be the light of a ghostly 'wrecker', trying to lure ships onto the rocks.

Old Lifeboat Station
Towan Head
Newquay TR7 1HN

41. THE OLD ALBION INN, CRANTOCK

The village of Crantock came into being in the year 460 when some Irish hermits established an oratory there. Large parts of the village are now owned by the National Trust.

The inn, which is known to have been used by smugglers, is 400 years old. In the mid 19th century, some of the timbers from the HMS Coventry were used in the building of an extension. Outside the door is a lamp of the kind that would have been used by wreckers to lure ships onto the rocks.

In the main lounge there is a 'smuggler's hole' (now blocked off) that leads from the fireplace into a tunnel that runs through the whole village and ends at the river. Some time ago, human bones were found in the tunnel but whether they belonged to someone who died there or to a body that was hidden there after being killed is unclear.

THE GHOSTS OF THE OLD ALBION INN

People have heard their names being called by disembodied voices, and three ghosts have been seen. One is a man in a brown frock coat and another is a young boy who is thought to have lived in the early 18th century. There is also a ghost who is said either to have been a smuggler or a sailor who died aboard the HMS Coventry and who came to the inn with the timbers used for the extension.

The Old Albion Inn
Langurroc Road
Crantock TR8 5RB
'phone: 01637 830243
website: www.oldalbioncrantock.com/

The inn serves food, and free WiFi is available.

42. THE SMUGGLERS DEN INN, TREBELLAN

This thatched inn was built in the 16th century and was a haunt of smugglers. Several smugglers are said still to haunt the building, including one known as Black Face Kelly. Legend says that he was a vicious man who eventually disappeared, together with a large amount of gold. But there's no indication as to whether he disappeared of his own free will in order to enjoy his ill gotten gains or whether someone killed him and stole the gold.

The Smugglers Den Inn
Trebellan TR85PY
'phone: 01637 830209
website: www.thesmugglersden.co.uk/
email: Hello@thesmugglersden.co.uk

Look out for signs to the Smugglers' Den as the postcode won't work on some SatNavs. The inn serves food and is wheelchair accessible.

43. WHEAL COATES MINE, ST AGNES

Wheal Coates mine was worked between 1802 and 1889 and, again, between 1911 and 1913 after which it closed for good. One of its three engine houses, Towanroath Shaft, is now a Grade II listed building. The whole site and the adjacent Chapel Porth beach is owned by the National Trust.

THE GHOSTS OF WHEAL COATES

It is said that the mine is haunted by the ghosts of some of the miners who died there. Visitors to the site have reported hearing voices whispering, particularly when the weather is cold and windy.

Wheal Coates Mine
Beacon Drive
St Agnes TR5 0NT

The mine shaft is accessible at low tide via a large cave at the far end of Chapel Porth beach. BUT it is vital that, if you visit it, you wear sturdy, flat shoes and make yourself aware of the tides because the sea can come in very quickly and it's all too easy to find yourself cut off.

44. PORTREATH

44a. The Waterfront Inn

Before the inn was built, there was another building on this site – and it was here that people brought the bodies washed up on the shore following a shipwreck. The bodies were laid out with a label as to the date on which they were found in the hope that their relatives, learning that their loved one had been lost in the wreck, would come and be able to identify the body.

The ghost, who has been seen by many people over the years, is that of a man who seems to be waiting for someone. Perhaps he was one of those who lost his life in a shipwreck and is still waiting for his family to find him.

The Waterfront Inn
Forth an Nance
Portreath TR16 4NQ
'phone: 01209 842777
website: https://thewaterfrontinn.webs.com/
email: clemtregear@aol.co.uk

The Waterfront Inn serves food and is wheelchair accessible.

44b. The Basset Arms

Ghostly figures have been seen in several places around the pub and objects have been observed to move by themselves. In the lounge bar a figure is often seen walking through the wall at the place where a door used to be.

The Basset Arms
Tregea Terrace
Portreath TR16 4NG
'phone: 01209 842077
website: www.thebassetarms-portreath.foodand
drinksites.co.uk/
email: bassetarms@btconnect.com

The Basset Arms serves food and is wheelchair accessible. Free WiFi is available.

44c. Portreath Arms Hotel

There is just one ghost at the Portreath Arms – that of a woman who haunts the lounge bar and the ladies' room.

Portreath Arms Hotel
The Square
Portreath TR16 4LA
'phone: 01209 842 259

website: www.theportreatharms.co.uk/
email: email@theportreatharms.co.uk

A family owned hotel, the Portreath Arms has seven bedrooms and is pet friendly.

44d. Smugglers Cottage

In the mid 20th century, a concealed room was discovered in the 16th century cottage that stood on this site. In the room was the skeleton of a man in a black cloak, together with a sword and an old sea chest. It seemed likely that the man had been a smuggler but there was no indication as to how he became trapped there. However, the discovery was thought to explain the ghost that people had been seeing around the cottage for about 300 years. Whether the ghost still haunts here is uncertain, as the cottage has since been demolished and rebuilt.

Smugglers Cove Cottages
Smugglers Cove
Portreath TR16 4NS
'phone: 07768 602498
website: https://smugglerscovecottages.com/
email: stay@smugglerscovecottages.com

The new building offers self-catering accommodation.

45. TRURO

Although Truro is Cornwall's only city, it's not Cornwall's county town (that is Bodmin). It has been a market town and a port for more than 800 years and was a centre of tin mining for many years. There are, however, very few buildings left that date to its early years – most of the town centre was built in the 18th and 19th centuries.

Many stories are told of highwaymen, smugglers and press gangs in Truro and, perhaps as a result of its violent history, it is now said to be one of the most haunted places in Cornwall.

45a. Devil's Arch Bridge

Turn east into St. Clement's Hill from the large roundabout on the A390 in the centre of Truro (just north east of the bus station and the river) and continue along it towards Tresillian for about a mile and a half, and you will come to a low, narrow bridge. This is the Devil's Arch bridge – so called because legend has it that, if you walk under it without holding your breath, the devil will seize you and drag you into hell. Presumably driving under it without holding your breath doesn't incur the same penalty – although it is a well known spot for lorries to get stuck!

THE GHOSTS OF THE DEVIL'S ARCH BRIDGE

It's said that there was a highwayman who would stand on the bridge dangling a noose in order to stop coaches by ensnaring their drivers, and his ghost is still there .

Some people have heard the sound of horses galloping up the road, without actually seeing anything, while others have seen a man on horseback or a horse-drawn coach.

During the Civil War, Royalist soldiers who were captured at Tresilian, where they had made their last stand, were taken to the bridge to be hanged. They have been seen there by a number of people.

And a man and woman in Victorian dress are sometimes seen – she is dressed all in white while he wears a top hat and carries a walking cane.

45b. Comprigney Hill

Comprigney Hill is a short, narrow road which turns south off the B3284 at Kenwyn. The word Comprigney is derived from the Cornish *gweal clogh prennyer* which means 'gallows field'. Somewhere to the side of this road there used to be a gibbet where men were hanged and their bodies left to rot. At night, it is said that you can still hear the rattling of chains and see shadowy figures around the place where the gibbet once stood.

45c. The Wig and Pen

The pub is haunted by a girl who, it is said, was murdered either here or somewhere nearby. She tends to be seen in the late evening.

The Wig and Pen
1 Frances Street
Truro TR1 3DP
'phone: 01872 713039
website: www.thewigandpentruro.co.uk/

Situated in the heart of Truro, the Wig and Pen serves food and is wheelchair accessible.

45d. The William the Fourth

This city centre pub was built on the site of a former Dominican friary. One of the Dominican friars has evidently found it hard to leave and is still seen around the building.

The William the Fourth

5/6 Kenwyn Street, Truro TR1 3DJ

'phone: 01872 273334

website: https://thewilliamivtruro.co.uk/

email: info@thewilliamivtruro.co.uk

The pub serves food and is wheelchair accessible. Free WiFi is available as well as free off-street parking.

45e. The Old Globe Bistro (formerly the Globe Public House)

The Globe pub closed in 2011 and was replaced by Reeds's Pharmacy and the Old Globe bistro. The building itself dates from the early 19th century and is said to be haunted by a young woman called Alice. Alice had the misfortune to be knocked down by a horse and cart in the street outside and was brought into the pub, where she died.

The Old Globe Bistro

24 Frances Street

Truro TR1 3DP

'phone: 01872 245149

email: theoldglobe@aol.com.

46. PENDENNIS CASTLE, FALMOUTH

Pendennis Castle and St. Mawes Castle were built in the first half of the 16th century to protect the Fal estuary from invasion by French or Spanish forces. Towards the end of the century, stone ramparts and a bastion were added. In the 1730s Pendennis Castle was modernised and upgraded and, in the 1790s, it was refortified. It was used by the armed forces in both World Wars and was finally decommissioned in 1956. It is now managed by English Heritage.

During the Civil War, the castle was initially held by a 1,000-strong Royalist garrison but in 1646, after a three month siege, it was captured by the Parliamentarians.

THE GHOSTS OF PENDENNIS CASTLE

The castle is said to have at least eight ghosts, although most of them are heard rather than seen.

As you walk up or down the stone staircases, you may be aware of other footsteps – those of the soldiers who were stationed here long ago. And in some of the rooms you may hear the sound of a child laughing coming from a dark corner. A long-dead Lieutenant Governor of the castle is also said to roam his old domain. And the sound of horses' hooves is sometimes heard – possibly those horses whom the starving Royalists were forced to kill and eat during the three month siege.

But perhaps the ghost most frequently encountered is that of a woman known as Maud. Some accounts describe her as a head cook but, more often, she is said to have been a kitchen maid. How she died is also uncertain – according to which story you read, she fell to her death either down some stairs while carrying a tray of food or from the ramparts as she hauled up a pot of gruel to feed the besieged troops. It is possible, however, that the fact of her carrying food was just introduced to the story at some time to explain her presence somewhere other than the kitchen. Her screams as she falls have been heard on numerous occasions and some people have claimed to have seen her body, lying where it fell.

Pendennis Castle
Castle Drive
Falmouth TR11 4LP
'phone: 01326 316594
website: www.english-heritage.org.uk/visit/places/pendennis-castle/

Visitors to the castle are able to see various reconstructions showing what castle life was like during different periods in its history.

47. PENRYN

The town of Penryn was well established by the mid 13th century when Henry III granted it a charter to hold a weekly market. It rapidly became a busy port and, by the 18th century, had developed into an important commercial centre.

47a. The Church of St Gluvias

The church tower dates back to the 15th century but parts of the building were restored in the late 19th century (the barrel shaped roof was left unchanged). In the 1950s, the Victorian chancel was lowered to its original proportions, the floor was laid with slate headstones and the walls were whitened.

THE GHOST OF THE CHURCH OF ST GLUVIAS

A former bell ringer at the church became a seaman and rose to the position of captain, but eventually he drowned while on a voyage. He is sometimes seen standing in the church and, occasionally, he rings the church bells in the early hours of the morning.

The Church of St Gluvias
Church Road
Penryn TR10 8AJ

47b. In and around Penryn

If you happen to be in Penryn just before Christmas you may see a phantom coach, drawn by headless horses. Be warned – just glance and look away. Local tradition says that, if you look straight at it, it may take you away with it.

48. KENNAL VALE

This deep valley between Falmouth and Redruth once housed one of the largest gunpowder factories in the country. There were about 50 buildings, widely spaced along the river bank, and the remains of a number of these – including the corning house, the mixing house, the packing house and the change house – can still be seen. Sections of some of the incorporating mills where the gunpowder was mixed and ground also remain. Much of what the factory produced was used in Cornish mines. But by the start of the First World War, mines and quarries were tending to use dynamite and gelignite, which were newer and safer than gunpowder, and the factory closed. Kennal Vale is now a nature reserve, managed by the Cornwall Wildlife Trust.

THE GHOSTS OF KENNAL VALE

People have reported seeing mill workers around the old buildings, including one man who stands and stares at those who walk past him but who vanishes if he is approached. One of the most frequently seen ghosts is said to be that of William Dunstan who died in an explosion in the press house in 1887, leaving a widow and ten children. A shadowy figure with poorly defined facial features is also said to roam around the buildings.

Some people have felt someone touch them as they enter a building. Blue and yellow orbs are often seen on photographs of the abandoned buildings, and many people have described a feeling of "a presence" being there.

Some visitors seem to have experienced time slips, suddenly becoming aware that they are looking at the factory buildings as they were in their heyday. And dogs have shown an unwillingness to walk in certain parts of the vale.

Kennal Vale
Ponsanooth TR3 7HJ

49. LANNER

This area is believed to have been inhabited since the Bronze Age and the village of Lanner was certainly established by the first half of the 16th century. It grew rapidly during the 19th century because of the local tin and copper mines.

THE GHOST OF LANNER

Near Murtons Terrace there is a footpath with a stile leading to it. Somewhere in this area, in the late 19th century, a little girl is said to have been trampled to death by horses. She appears from time to time near the stile.

Murtons Terrace
Lanner TR16 6HW

50. THE VICTORIA INN, FOUR LANES

The inn was built some 700 years ago but its ghosts date back to an incident in 1640 when some soldiers, fighting on the Parliamentarian side in the Civil War, were murdered here.

The Victoria Inn
1 The Square
Four Lanes TR16 6PZ
'phone: 07523 880956
website: http://victoriainnfourlanes.co.uk/
email: thevicfourlanes@aol.com

51. CAMBORNE

There has probably been a settlement in this area from Roman times. The remains of what is thought to have been a Romano-British villa, the only one of its kind known in Cornwall, were found near Camborne in 1931. There are also early Christian sites dating back to the 10th or 11th centuries and it is said that there used to be a pilgrimage chapel and a holy well locally.

Camborne became a centre of the tin and copper mining industry in the late 18th and early 19th centuries, although mining was first recorded in the area in the 1400s. It went on to become one of the richest tin mining areas in the world and was home to the Camborne School of Mines. Dolcoath mine, which closed in 1921 was, for a long time, the deepest mine in the world and South Crofty mine was the last working tin mine in Europe, closing in 1998.

THE GHOSTS OF CAMBORNE

Several sources refer to an unpublished paper by local historian F.J. Stephens entitled *Contributions to the Early History of the Parish of Camborne* in which the author commented that Camborne had always been famous for its ghosts, and went on to list several haunted sites. While no date is given for the paper, it seems likely that it was written in the mid- or late 19th century. Since then, some of the sites have disappeared but three are still identifiable.

The first of these was Bell Gate which is described as being "just outside Praze-An-Beeble near Vellan Saundry". While its exact location is unclear, this would have been somewhere along the two mile stretch of road that runs between Praze-An-Beeble (located where the B3280 crosses the B3303 south of Camborne) and Vellynsaundry House which lies just south of the Shire Inn, higher up the B3303. Stephens declared that there were numerous ghosts here and they used to be seen going in and out of an ancient cottage "which stood there once". Clearly the cottage had been demolished by the time Stephens was writing but whether the ghosts had dispersed as a result is uncertain.

Stephens also refers the reader to Knapp's Corner "at the turning down to Bareppa, near the railway bridge at the top of Pendarves Road". This is easier to pinpoint and clearly refers to the spot higher up the B3303 from Vellynsaundry, where the road crosses the railway. The ghost, says Stephens, would leap on people's backs and was of a vindictive nature.

Finally, an armed knight (sometimes referred to as an iron man) was occasionally seen " riding slowly up and down the valley between Reskadinnick and Menedarva". This road is now the A30 and it seems unlikely that the knight still rides there – but if you happen to be travelling along this section, keep an eye out for him!

51a. The Church of St Martin and St Meriadoc

This grade I listed church dates from the 15th century and is the parish church of Camborne. It was gutted and restored in the early 1860s and the outer south aisle was added in the late 1870s.

THE GHOSTS OF THE CHURCH OF ST MARTIN AND ST MERIADOC

Some years ago, two Camborne ladies who had been on a trip to Plymouth and had caught a late train back were walking home from the station around midnight. They passed the church and, as they did so, one lady saw two figures dressed in white appear by the church tower, walk silently through the churchyard gate and turn south into Rectory Road, where they vanished near Rectory Cottage. Admittedly, the other lady didn't see these figures, but perhaps that was because she was focused on a procession of ghostly figures wearing black, and with three cornered hats, coming from College Street, to the west.

The Church of St Martin and St Meriadoc

Church Street

Camborne TR14 7DF

51b. Reskadinnick House

This grade II listed building was probably built in the 17th century but there have been many alterations and additions and some restoration since then.

THE GHOST OF RESKADINNICK HOUSE

The house is said to be haunted by a member of the Vivian family who used to live here and he has been seen by passers-by, standing at one of the windows.

Reskadinnick House
Puggis Hill
Camborne TR14 0BH

Although it is not officially open to the public, the owners offer Air B&B.

52. THE CHURCH OF ST JOHN THE EVANGELIST, TRESLOTHAN

This little church was originally built in 1841 for the mine-owning Pendarves family, as the chapel to Pendarves House. The house was demolished in 1955 and its site is now a nature reserve known as Pendarves woods. The church, however, still stands and continues to be used. It is a grade II listed building.

THE GHOST OF THE CHURCH OF ST JOHN THE EVANGELIST

The ghost is said to be that of a lady who married into the Pendarves family and who rejoiced in the name of Tryphena Trist. In 1804 she married Edward William Wynne Stackhouse who inherited the Pendarves estate in 1819 and adopted the Pendarves surname. Edward became the MP for West Cornwall in 1832 and, ten years later, employed the architect George Wightwick to build him a church and mausoleum at Treslothan, where he had created a new estate for the mine workers.

Edward died in 1853 but Tryphena lived for another twenty years, finally dying at the age of 94. There is uncertainty as to whether her body lies with that of her husband in the family mausoleum. A headstone states that she does but, over the years, rumours have circulated that she was not buried there because of "unspecified misdemeanors". Whatever the truth of this, her ghost, dressed in white, has been seen in the graveyard and in the gardens of the nearby rectory.

The Church of St John the Evangelist
Treslothan TR14 9LP

53. GWITHIAN

This village is named after an Irish saint who built a church here in 490. The present church dates from the 15th century. Just to the north of the village is the Red River, so called because, when the mines near Camborne and Redruth were active, the water was coloured red by the tin residues released into it. Since the closure of the last mine in the 1990s, the river has lost its colour.

THE GHOST OF GWITHIAN

The ghost is that of a man who was so distraught after he found his home burned down and his sister missing that he jumped off the cliffs in the area known as Hell's Mouth. His screams can still be heard when the weather is stormy.

54. THE ROYAL STANDARD PUB, GWINEAR

This pub, which was originally a mining counthouse, was damaged by fire several years ago and has since been refurbished.

THE GHOST OF THE ROYAL STANDARD PUB

Disembodied footsteps and other strange noises have been heard around the pub and these are said to be caused by a lady known as Clare.

The Royal Standard Pub

50 Churchtown

Gwinear TR27 5JL

'phone: 01736 850080

website: www.royalstandardgwinear.co.uk/

The pub serves food and is wheelchair accessible. Free WiFi is available.

55. THE BUCKET OF BLOOD INN, PHILLACK

There are several stories as to the origin of the pub's name. The most popular says that, in time gone by, the landlord went out to the well to draw some water – and pulled up a bucket filled with blood. On investigation, it was found that the murdered body of an Customs officer, who was on the trail of some local smugglers, had been thrown down there. A variant of this story is that the man was not himself an Customs officer but an informer who had been tipping off the authorities. Another, less dramatic explanation, says that the water only looked like blood because it had been coloured by residues from the local tin mine.

The pub itself is said to have been built on the site of a 12th century monastery and may incorporate some of the original building.

THE GHOSTS OF THE BUCKET OF BLOOD INN

A monk, presumably one of those from the 12th century monastery, has been seen in the darker corners of the pub. From time to time staff find that furniture has been moved around during the night and this has been put down to the monk. It is possible that he is also responsible for the prod in the back that some people have experienced in the bar.

The man in the well also makes an occasional appearance in the public bar, still dressed in his torn, wet clothes.

In addition, a former customer named Jack, who died in 1972, has been known to return and to sit in one of the booths having a pint of beer before vanishing.

Ghostly figures have been seen crossing the road outside the pub, while inside the building disembodied footsteps are sometimes heard.

The Bucket of Blood Inn
14 Church Town Road
Phillack TR27 5AE
'phone: 01736 447928
website: www.staustellbrewery.co.uk/pub/phillack/bucket-of-blood

Pub food is available.

56. ST IVES

There is thought to have been a settlement here as early as the Bronze Age and it has been a busy fishing port since the Middle Ages. Many well known artists have worked here, including Bernard Leach, Ben Nicholson and Barbara Hepworth and the town now hosts a branch of the Tate Gallery and the Barbara Hepworth Museum.

56a. Street-an-pol

Known as Dead Man's Walk, this narrow lane leads past the Guildhall and is said to be the road down which condemned prisoners were marched to their place of execution.

Walking down here, people have heard disembodied footsteps and the clanking of chains, have seen shadowy figures, and have felt a tightening around their necks as though from a rope.

Street-an-pol
St Ives TR26 2DS

56b. The Regent Hotel

Originally the house of a ship's captain, the Regent became a hotel in 1936 and, for more than 30 years, has been run by one family.

THE GHOSTS OF THE REGENT HOTEL

Guests often hear sounds of loud knocking and of furniture being moved. A short elderly man, thought to have been the superintendent of the nearby mine, is frequently seen around the hotel as are a young boy (believed to be a stable boy) and a chambermaid. A man in uniform is often seen standing at the foot of the stairs. He looks so unlike a ghost that some people speak to him – which seems to be his cue to vanish!

The Regent Hotel
Fernlea Terrace
St Ives TR26 2BH
'phone: 01736 796195
website: www.hotelinstives.com/

56c. Island Road

This road, which leads down to Porthgwidden Beach, is haunted by a horse and his owner. The story is that, about 200 years ago, a certain Mr. Birch would ride his white horse down to the beach every evening in order to have a swim.

But one evening he didn't return from his swim and his horse was later found, still on the beach, patiently waiting. The horse was taken in by a local stables and, after he died some years later, the apparitions began. The horse would be seen trotting down Island Road and returning carrying his owner. Nowadays, they don't appear so often but many people still hear hoof beats at dusk.

Island Road
St Ives TR26 1NT

56d. St Ives Bay

A ghost ship has been seen off St Ives Head many times. The sound of bells has been heard coming from the deep water and, before a storm, lights are often seen out to sea.

Another light is also seen in St Ives Bay on stormy nights. It is carried by 'the Lady with the Lantern' whose baby was swept out to sea during a storm. One tradition says that she is looking for her baby, while another says she is trying to warn ships that they risk being wrecked on the shore.

57. TRENCROM (OR TRECOBBEN) HILLFORT

This Iron Age fort is said to be haunted by the ghosts of its original inhabitants. If you walk up here, you may feel that you are being watched and, if you have a dog with you, don't be surprised if he seems to want to protect you from something you can't see.

Trencrom Hill Fort
Ludgvan TR27 6NX

58. ZENNOR

Zennor is an interesting village on several counts. It has an industrial heritage – granite from a local quarry was used to build the walls of Falmouth Harbour and much of St Ives. It also has a linguistic heritage – it was one of the last places where you could have heard the Cornish language spoken. Archaeological interest is provided by a dolmen and a burial chamber, known as Zennor Quoit, high up on the moor with, beside it, the remains of a cow shed masquerading as five standing stones! And it has a local legend about a mermaid which is recorded in the parish church. The story goes that this mermaid enticed the son of a churchwarden into the sea and he never returned. But, oddly, it is not the churchwarden's son but the mermaid who is commemorated in the church, with a carving of her on a mediaeval bench end and an image of her on a bronze dial, dated 1737, on the side of the church tower.

58a. The Road to Foage Farm

Across the B3306 from Zennor and running from a point almost opposite the more easterly of the two roads into the village, lies a one mile long public footpath leading to Foage Farm, which was built in the late 19th century.

THE GHOST OF THE ROAD TO FOAGE FARM

The road is haunted by a man on a bicycle. He is dressed in Victorian clothes, is covered in blood and pedals at speed down the narrow lane. He is believed to have been a miner who was killed in an explosion. A video on YouTube takes the viewer down this lane but, sadly, the ghost does not put in an appearance – just a black cat.

Foage Farm
Zennor TR26 3BU

58b. The Tinner's Arms

The building dates back to 1271 when it was erected to house the stonemasons who were building the Church of St Senara.

THE GHOST OF THE TINNER'S ARMS

The ghost of a miner has been seen by a number of people, standing outside the main door of the pub. There is also a poltergeist who tends to be active just before a storm and who moves glasses and knocks pictures from the walls.

The Tinner's Arms

Zennor TR26 3BY

'phone: 01736 796927

website: https://tinnersarms.com/

email: enquiries@tinnersarms.co.uk

59. CHYSAUSTER

This is one of the best preserved Iron Age villages in Britain. It is thought to have been built by members of the Dumonii tribe around 100BC and to have been in use for four or five hundred years.

It consists of about ten so-called 'courtyard houses', a style found only on the Land's End peninsula and the Isles of Scilly. Each house would have consisted of several thatched rooms around an open central courtyard. The village has been the subject of several excavations and reconstructions.

THE GHOSTS OF CHYSAUSTER

Small ghostly men, thought to have been the original Iron Age settlers, are sometimes seen around the village.

Chysauster
Newmill TR20 8XA

Chysauster is signposted from Gulval. There is a small entry fee.

60. THE CHURCH OF ST PAUL, LUDGVAN

The original church here was Norman but, in the 15th century, it was rebuilt and the tower was added. In 1761 considerable damage occurred when the building was struck by lightning – both the pulpit and the communion table were shattered.

THE GHOSTS OF THE CHURCH OF ST PAUL

For many years people have been seeing a very tall figure, wrapped in what appears to be a white shroud, walking in the churchyard and then disappearing into a wall. It is thought to be the ghost of Sarah Polgrean who, in 1820, was hanged for the murder of her husband. Sarah had, apparently, had a number of lovers but fell in love with a sailor named Jack and it seems that he was the reason she decided that her husband had to go. At first, her husband's death was accepted as having been due to natural causes since he was considerably older than she was. But rumours started to spread when she paired up with Jack immediately after the funeral – so much so that an exhumation of the body was ordered. A post mortem examination revealed a large quantity of arsenic in Mr Polgrean's body, and Sarah was arrested.

Condemned to death, Sarah's last request was that Jack would walk with her to the scaffold. Once there, they kissed, and people standing nearby heard her say "You promise – you will?" to which Jack replied "I will, Sarah, I will."

Soon after the execution, Sarah's ghost started to be seen in Ludgvan, sometimes on the road between Penzance and Hayle, and sometimes in the churchyard. She appeared frequently to Jack who started to look haggard and distressed. He told friends that the promise he made on the scaffold was to marry Sarah, either alive or dead. On the anniversary of her death, Jack was at sea. Accounts vary as to what happened – one says that, around midnight, the crew heard a woman's footsteps walking towards the place where Jack slept and that he got up, climbed up on deck and threw himself overboard, and as the sea swallowed him up, his shipmates heard the sound of church bells. Another account, however, says that there was a great storm, during which church bells could be heard, and that Jack was swept overboard by a huge wave.

A ghostly couple is also seen in the churchyard from time to time, but whether they are Sarah and Jack or another pair of lovers is unclear.

During storms, sailors have heard a voice saying "I will, I will". Phantom bells can still sometimes be heard at midnight, far out in Mount's Bay, which is the great bay that stretches from Gwennap Head in the west to Lizard Point in the east.

The Church of St Paul

Ludgvan TR20 8HA

61. PRIEST COVE

In the 19th century, copper and tin were mined here and the entrances to the tunnels that were dug can still be seen, fenced off, at the back of the beach. Before this, the beach was the site of a more nefarious industry – that of wrecking. Wreckers would set lights up on the shore to masquerade as the lights of a harbour. Ships would be lured onto the rocks and the wreckers would steal their cargoes as they sank.

The ghost associated with this cove is seen out at sea, holding onto a plank of wood to stop himself from sinking. It is said that he was, himself, a wrecker, but he might equally be one of the wreckers' victims.

Priest Cove
Cape Cornwall
St Just in Penwith TR19 7NN

62. ST JUST

St Just is the nearest town to Land's End and, as the abandoned engine houses make clear, it was once an important mining centre. Both the church and the pub next to it date back to the 14th century and the town is surrounded by prehistoric sites. A number of these, including the 19 standing stones of the Tregeseal stone circle, are on the hill known as Carn Kenidjack.

THE GHOSTS OF ST JUST

Carn Kenidjack is said to be haunted by a woman in a red shawl who used to terrorize miners as they walked to and from their work.

Just off the B3306 immediately north of St Just, a narrow road runs east towards Tregeseal. It is said that, on stormy nights, the sound of a horse drawn carriage can be heard here.

63. LAND'S END

As well as being a major tourist attraction, Land's End is the point where the north coastal footpath meets that of the south coast, joining Poole Harbour (in Dorset) to the Bristol Channel and covering over 500 miles.

THE GHOSTS OF LAND'S END

If you stand at Land's End at midnight, you may hear bells tolling. They are said to be rung by a ship's captain who was lost at sea but who refuses to believe that his ship has sunk.

Lands End TR19 7AA.

There is a theme park at Land's End which covers everything from the lost land of Lyonesse and King Arthur to present day Cornwall. Car parking incurs a fee (at a reduced rate if you don't want to visit the theme park). Buses run all year from Penzance and, in the summer, from St. Ives.

64. SENNEN

64a. The First and Last Inn

Built in the 17th century, this inn was once the haunt of smugglers and wreckers.

THE GHOST OF THE FIRST AND LAST INN

In the early 19th century, smuggling was rife and one of the people at the centre of this was local farmer Dionysius Williams who was also the owner of the First and Last Inn. The day to day management of the inn was carried out by a married couple, Annie and Joseph George who were also well acquainted with smuggling. When, in 1805, Joseph's brother John was tried for organising a gang whose purpose was to take back contraband which had been seized by Customs officers, Annie gave evidence against him. As a result, John was found guilty and hanged.

Legend says that this was not the first time that Annie had spoken out about the smugglers. But, unfortunately, she did not do this from the best of motives. Having tried, unsuccessfully, to get Dionysius Williams to allow her and her husband to have the inn rent free, Annie betrayed him to the authorities. Her vindictive streak continued to be demonstrated with other people against whom she gave evidence, and it is said that her betrayal of her brother-in-law John happened following an argument about a tobacco deal, where she didn't get her own way.

Eventually the villagers, having decided that enough was enough, dragged her out to the beach at low tide, tied her to some stakes, covered her with fishing nets and left her to drown as the water rose. Her body was brought back to the inn before being buried in an unmarked grave in St Sennan churchyard.

Annie, dressed all in black, has been seen around the inn on many occasions. And she still has her vindictive nature – if the landlord of the time has pets, she seems to enjoy trapping them in drawers and wardrobes. She brings a sudden chill with her and some people have felt her touch their hair. She is also known to move things around and knock glasses off the shelves.

The First and Last Inn
Lands End Road
Sennen TR19 7AD
'phone: 01736 871680.
website: www.firstandlastinn.co.uk/

The inn serves food, is wheelchair accessible and offers free WiFi.

64b. Irish Lady Rock, Sennen Cove

The beach at Sennen Cove is known as Whitesands Bay because it has one of the finest stretches of sand in Cornwall. It is a popular spot for surfers but it has not always been a happy place. When a ship ran aground here many years ago, everyone on board was lost, including one woman who managed to hold onto a rock for two hours but drowned before she could be rescued. It is her ghost that is sometimes seen, still clinging to the rocks around the bay.

65. ST LEVAN

The village boasts a 12th century church, a holy well and the remains of an ancient chapel.

THE GHOSTS OF ST LEVAN

Legend says that, many years ago, a man who lived in St Levan would row out to sea in a small boat with his servant, returning at dusk. No one knew anything about either the man or his servant. Eventually the master died and, as he was being buried in St Levan churchyard, his servant vanished into thin air. The two men are thought to be associated with the ghostly galleon which has been seen heading towards the shore and then continuing overland before disappearing near St Levan.

66. HELLA POINT

Hella Point lies due south of Porthgwarra and it is said that a farmer's daughter who lived locally used to stand here every day, waiting for her seafaring lover to return. One night she heard him calling her, went out to the Point and was never seen again. News came later that he had drowned that same night. The two lovers are thought still to haunt the spot where she was last seen.

Hella Point
Porthgwarra TR19 6JR

67. THE SHIP INN, MOUSEHOLE

The village of Mousehole (described by Dylan Thomas as the loveliest village in England) is mentioned in records dating back to the 13th century when it was an important fishing port.

THE GHOST OF THE SHIP INN

A man has been seen around the inn, variously described as leaning against a wall, walking along a corridor at an angle as though on a ship, and disappearing when spoken to.

The Ship Inn
Mousehole TR19 6QX.
'phone: 01736 731234
website: https://shipinnmousehole.co.uk/

The Ship Inn overlooks the harbour. It serves food and free WiFi is available.

68. PENZANCE

Penzance has been a commercial centre for many centuries. It has what is thought to be the oldest Georgian theatre still standing in the country (built around 1786), and most of the buildings in Chapel Street date from the late 18th century. The Admiral Benbow pub dates, in part, from the 17th century, while the Turks Head is thought to have been built in 1233. The earliest structure, however, is the Iron Age hill fort known as Lescudjack Castle which is a scheduled ancient monument and consists of a single rampart surrounding 3 acres of land.

68a. Penzance Cemetery

A number of people have reported seeing ghostly forms floating around the cemetery, especially after dark.

Penzance Cemetery
Nancealverne
Heamoor, TR18 2PH

68b. Castle Horneck

The site on which this Georgian mansion was built is thought originally to have housed an Iron Age settlement, followed by a mediaeval castle and then an Elizabethan manor house. It was for many years the home of the Borlase family and is now a Youth Hostel.

THE GHOSTS OF CASTLE HORNECK

Lady Margaret Borlase is said to haunt the building, together with some of her 14 children, whose laughter and footsteps have been heard. George Borlase, who inherited the manor in 1839, also remains on the premises. A dark shadowy form, known to the hostel staff as Edward, is frequently seen walking into the storerooms, while another, taller, shadowy man has been seen apparently guarding the door of the hostel. There is also said to be a phantom dog roaming around.

From the outside, a woman has been observed several times at one of the windows, while sometimes a coach and horses is seen coming up the drive at midnight.

Castle Horneck

Penzance TR20 8TF

'phone: 03453 719653

website: www.yha.org.uk/hostel/yha-penzance

email: penzance@yha.org.uk

The Youth Hostel has private rooms available.

68c. Co-op Store, Queen's Square

Unusually, this is a haunted supermarket! Disembodied footsteps have been heard and, after closing time, things have been moved around – and a CCTV camera recorded a pack of beer being thrown off the shelf by invisible hands.

The Co-op
Queen's Square TR18 2JJ

68d. Pengersick Castle

The oldest part of the castle dates back to the early 16th century although the Pengersick family has lived on this site since the 12th century.

THE GHOSTS OF PENGERSICK CASTLE

The castle has been called one of the most haunted places in Cornwall. A hooded figure has been seen many times, particularly in the mediaeval garden, and is thought to be the ghost of a monk who came to collect the tithes due to the church but was killed by the castle's original owner, Henry Pengersick. Henry was later excommunicated for this savage act. Henry's wife, Engrina, is seen around the castle, particularly in the main bedroom which she shares with two other ghosts. One of these is a woman who tends to materialise by the window in the early hours and then, after looking out for a minute or two, lies down on the bed and starts to writhe in agony, while another ghostly woman appears through the wall to stand by her bedside. What the story is of these two women, no one is sure although the second woman is thought to have been a servant.

There is a crusader who wears a traditional white tabard emblazoned with a red cross, and a ghost on the battlements, said to have been a certain John Milliton who, in the early 16th century, put poison in his wife's goblet - but ended up drinking it himself after she switched the cups around when he wasn't looking.

The many other ghosts include a young girl, a cat, a dog and a number of phantom rats!

Pengersick Castle
Praa Sands
Penzance TR20 9SJ
'phone: 01736 763 973
website: www.pengersickcastle.com/
email: chairman@pengersickcastle.org.uk

The Castle is now a wedding and events venue but it is open for tours by appointment.

68e. Chapel Street

Several ghosts haunt Chapel Street. One is said to be that of a certain Mrs Baines who lived in the street, in a house with an apple orchard. Local children did what children have been doing since time immemorial and sneaked into the orchard to steal apples. This infuriated Mrs Baines so much that she employed a man named Jan to keep watch. And one night, to check on how well he was doing this, she crept into the orchard. Unfortunately, Jan had fallen asleep and Mrs Baines' sudden appearance woke him, startling him so much that he accidently fired the gun he held – and Mrs Baines was killed (although some versions of the story say that she wasn't hit but her death occurred shortly afterwards, from shock). Since then, her ghost has taken up residence in the Turks Head pub, although she has also been seen elsewhere in Chapel Street, still dressed in the nightgown and lace cap in which she died.

In addition to Mrs Baines, ghostly funeral processions have been seen making their way towards St. Mary's church-yard at the bottom of the street. And a coach drawn by headless horses has frequently been reported driving down the street at midnight. The stories behind these last two hauntings are unknown.

Chapel Street
Penzance TR18 4AQ

68f. The Dolphin Tavern

Built about 500 years ago, the Dolphin Tavern has long been popular with sailors and, in the late 16th century, was used by Sir John Hawkins as a base from which to recruit men to fight the Spanish Armada. A century later it was transformed into a temporary courtroom where the infamous Judge Jeffreys tried those who supported the Duke of Monmouth's rebellion.

THE GHOSTS OF THE DOLPHIN TAVERN

There are at least three ghosts who have been seen regularly. One is an old sea captain, nicknamed George, who wears a tricorn hat, lace ruffles and a coat with brass buttons. He wanders around the upstairs rooms and corridors but is more often heard than seen. Legend says that either he was sentenced to hang by Judge Jeffreys for a minor crime, or that he was a smuggler who keeps coming back, trying to find his hidden contraband.

A younger, fair haired man also prowls the upper corridor and the stairs. Several landlords and landladies have woken up to find him in their bedroom, sometimes even sitting on the bed! If he's spoken to, he simply drifts away. Who he is, no one knows for sure although it has been suggested that he was a man known to have died in 1873 after falling into the cellar.

The third ghost is a woman in a Victorian dress who materialises in the main bar, glides across the room and then disappears into the wall.

In addition, the sound of something heavy being dragged across a floor is occasionally heard and, in unoccupied bedrooms, the beds sometimes appear to have been slept in, despite the doors to the rooms being locked.

The Dolphin Tavern
Quay Street
Penzance TR18 4BD
'phone: 01736 364106
website: www.dolphintavern.co.uk/
email: dolphintavern@tiscali.co.uk

The tavern offers bed and breakfast, and serves food. Free WiFi is available.

69. ST MICHAEL'S MOUNT

An island with a mediaeval castle in the middle of Mount's Bay, St Michael's Mount has, for centuries, been the home of the St Aubyn family, and is now managed by the National Trust. The only access at high tide is by boat although, when the tide is out, there is a causeway to the mainland.

At one time, there was a priory on the island but in 1193 the Mount was seized by Henry de la Pomeray, and it was he who started building the castle. In 1659 it was bought by Colonel St Aubyn. The grounds of the castle boast exotic gardens which were first planted in the late 18th century. During the 19th century, the harbour was in constant use and the population of the island rose to around 300. Nowadays some 30 people live on the island.

THE GHOSTS OF ST MICHAEL'S MOUNT

A phantom monk has been seen, dating back, no doubt, to the time when there was a priory on the island. There is also a lady in a grey dress, thought to have been the St Aubyn family's nanny in the mid 18th century. The legend is that she became pregnant but, when the father of her child rejected her, she threw herself from the battlements.

Out in the bay fishermen sometimes hear the sound of church bells and the voice of Sarah Polgrean's lover Jack (whose story is told above in section 60) whispering "I will, I will".

70. GODOLPHIN HOUSE

Godolphin House, formerly the seat of the Dukes of Leeds and the Earls of Godolphin, was built in the 16th century and is now owned by the National Trust. The formal gardens have hardly changed since they were created and form one of the most important historic gardens in Europe.

THE GHOSTS OF GODOLPHIN HOUSE

Margaret, wife of the first Earl of Godolphin, died in childbirth in 1678 at the age of 26. Since then, she has been seen in the house and gardens, and the rustle of her skirts has been heard around the house. Known as 'the white lady', she comes out of a closet in the entrance hall and walks onto the terrace and then into a tree-lined avenue that leads to the chapel. Her funeral procession, walking slowly towards the chapel on what is now known as 'the ghost path', has also been seen. She and her funeral are most likely to be seen on September 9th, which is the anniversary of her death.

Godolphin House
Godolphin Cross TR13 9RE
'phone: 01736763194

website: www.nationaltrust.org.uk/godolphin

email: godolphin@nationaltrust.org.uk

71. HELSTON

Helston is best known for Flora Day which is held every year on May 8th (or on the preceding Saturday if the 8th falls on a Sunday or Monday). The major event on Flora Day is the Furry Dance – a series of four dances whose origins are unknown but, most likely, are derived from a pre-Christian ritual celebrating the end of winter. The dances start at 7am with dancers in summer attire, followed by schoolchildren dressed in white and then, at midday, the 'gentry' with the women in long gowns and the men in morning dress and, finally, at 5pm, representatives of the town's tradesmen and women. The lead set of each dance is reserved for people born in Helston. At the same time, a street theatre, known as Hal an Tow, travels around the town performing a piece that probably originated in the Middle Ages, in which St George slays the dragon and St Michael banishes the Devil.

71a. The Angel Hotel

Dating from the 16th century, the hotel was once the town house of Lord Sidney Godolphin, one of the most important politicians in British history and husband of Lady Margaret

Godolphin whose ghost haunts Godolphin House (see section 70 above). In the 18th century it became a coaching inn. The hotel has one ghost – a woman known as Nelly, who wanders around the top floor.

The Angel Hotel
16 Coinagehall Street
Helston TR13 8EB
'phone: 01326 569393
website: http://angelhotelhelston.co.uk/
email: angelhotelhelston@gmail.com

The hotel is a good spot from which to view the Furry Dance.

71b. The Beehive Inn

Three ghosts have been reported here. One is a man in modern clothes. The second is an old lady who haunts the upper part of the inn. And the third is described as being seen only seen briefly "out of the corner of your eye".

The Beehive Inn
6 Coinagehall Street
Helston TR13 8SU
'phone: 01326 563995
website: www.facebook.com/Thebeehivehelston/
email: beehive.helston@gmail.com

72. POLDARK MINE

This mine lays claim to fame on several counts. Not only is it thought to be the deepest mine in the UK but it has what are believed to be the oldest complete mine workings in Great Britain that are open to the public. In addition, it is the only complete tin mine in Cornwall which offers guided tours and it is the only place in the UK with an underground post box with its own postmark.

Although there is clear evidence of mining from the 6th century or even earlier, the peak production of the mine – which was then called the Wheal Roots Mine – was in the 18th century when some 900 men and boys were employed here. But by the 20th century it had been abandoned. However, in 1972 a steam engine museum opened on the site and, in the course of construction, the mine was discovered. It was restored and its name changed to the Poldark Mine.

THE GHOSTS OF THE POLDARK MINE

Visitors have reported a number of experiences including strange noises echoing through the dark tunnels and an aggressive voice (thought to be that of a long dead miner) which swears at people and tells them to leave the mine.

Visitors who have taken photographs have seen strange mists on them or even an unidentifiable figure lurking in the shadows. At least one person has seen a figure materialise and then disappear.

Poldark Mine
Trenear
Wendron TR13 0ES
'phone: 01326 573173
website: www.poldarkmine.org.uk/index.php
email: info@poldarkmine.org.uk

The mine is on several levels and is not suitable for disabled visitors nor for those who suffer from claustrophobia as the tour goes down to a depth of 100 feet, up and down a number of flights of stairs and along winding, narrow, low roofed passages. Sensible shoes are essential and hard hats are provided.

73. CROFT PASCOE POOL

Croft Pascoe Pool – actually a small lake – is located on Goonhilly Downs, a Site of Special Scientific Interest on the Lizard peninsula, just south of Helston. The pool is at the centre of a bird-watcher's paradise – there are 78 species of birds to be found within a five mile radius.

THE GHOST OF CROFT PASCOE POOL

The ghost here is not so much a 'who' as a 'what'. A phantom sailing ship has been seen on many occasions, its sails bellowing, even on windless nights. It tends to appear mainly when the moon is full.

Croft Pascoe Pool
Goonhilly Downs TR12 6RW

74. CADGWITH COVE INN

This 300 year old inn lies on the Lizard Peninsula coastal walk and has two ghosts - one a fisherman and the other a smuggler. In addition, disembodied footsteps have been heard outside the inn.

Cadwith Cove Inn
Cadgwith TR12 7JX
'phone: 01326290513
website: www.cadgwithcoveinn.com/en-GB
email: garryandhelen@cadgwithcoveinn.co.uk

The inn has six bed and breakfast rooms. It serves food and free WiFi is available. Because of the age and location of the inn, there is no disabled access.

75. LIZARD

75a. Pistil Meadow

In 1721, the Royal Anne galley, a military transport heading for the West Indies, was swept against the cliffs during a storm. The number of people who died is uncertain – some accounts say it was 15, others say 200 or more. The bodies of these unfortunates were said to have been buried in Pistil Meadow but, since no evidence of a mass grave has been found, it seems likely that there were considerably fewer than 200.

Locals claim that the ghosts of those who are buried here haunt the meadow to this day.

Pistil Meadow
South West Coast Path TR12 7NU

75b. Housel Bay Hotel

During the Second World War, the hotel was commandeered by the RAF. In 1943 it was occupied by the WAAF Radar Plotting team whose commander was Flying Officer

William Croft. Despite being a married man, he fell deeply in love with Corporal Joan Lewis of the WAAF. The feelings, it seems, were mutual but, when their relationship became known, Joan was ordered to transfer to another posting. William and Joan could not bear to be parted and so made a suicide pact. However, this went wrong – William lived and Joan died – and William was put on trial for Joan's murder. Found guilty, he was sentenced to death but this was commuted to life imprisonment.

Since then, Joan has been seen on a number of occasions in the hotel gardens. Wearing her WAAF uniform, she sits on a bench, crying. One hotel guest, who was an artist, drew a likeness of Joan after seeing her sitting there, and another had a conversation with her and was told that she was waiting for her lover to join her.

Housel Bay Hotel
Lizard TR12 7PG
'phone: 01326 567500
website: www.houselbay.com/
email: stay@houselbay.com

Lightning Source UK Ltd.
Milton Keynes UK
UKHW020732161222
414034UK00018B/1453

9 781999 710781